Real Projects for Real People

The Patching Zone

Volume 1

Colophon
Editor *Anne Nigten*
Graphic Design *Bosenco.nl and Madi Kolpa*
Copy editing *Lyndsey Housden*
Publisher *V2_ publishing*
Distribution *NAi and V2_ Publishing, www.v2.nl*

Credits
All chapters of this book; on the theory and practice, were informed by our teams of talented
people, the commissioners, funding bodies, and mentors, The Patching Zone supervisory
board and the jury committees. We would like to thank all of them for the trust in these early
years of The Patching Zone adventure. We thank all contributors for their texts, visual material, pictures, input and ideas and all non-writers for making this possible.

This publication was made possible by financial support from Ministry of Economic Affairs
Ministry of Culture, Education and Science, Pact op Zuid / Rotterdam South Pact and Virtueel
Platform

ISBN: 9789056627973

www.patchingzone.net

Table of Contents

Patching
the Zones
Alex Adriaansens

Alex Adriaansens, director V2_,
Institute for the Unstable Media
Rotterdam (NL)

Some time ago Siegfried Zielinski (D)[1] initiated a performance dinner in Rotterdam called The Three Princes of Serendip. It showed how a good pasta pesto is made, not with an electric blender but by carefully choosing the ingredients and slowly mixing them by hand to get the optimum mix. The performance dinner metaphorically referred to the mingling of different sorts of knowledge and its productive potentials. Of course nobody knew in advance if the end result would be tasty but since Zielinski is an expert in the Italian kitchen we trusted him. During the dinner, Zielinski was telling a narrative that began in the late Middle Ages in monasteries, that explained the development of the first audio visual apparatuses by the monks, many of them forgotten in the meantime but they had a big impact on the apparatus as we know it today. The monasteries in those days were knowledge centers, since the church had collected all kind of 'dangerous' books in the libraries of these monasteries. The narrative of the development of the audio visual apparatus was mixed with the Persian story about 'The Three Princes of Serendip', where three princes were sent into the world by their father to learn about the world outside of the palace, the real world. While traveling the princes figured out a method of how to relate and combine the different sorts of information they were confronted with and how to interpret and build relations between these fragments of information. They learnt how to create meaning, how to get a good insight into the 'real' world, to be able to act and interact with it and shape it. From this story the concept of serendipity arose, which means discovering something while actually looking for something else.

The story above offers us a rich context to look at contemporary developments and insights in practices like art, science, culture and education. We come from a century focused on deep specialisation creating specific and separate knowledge domains. This approach gave us an abstract and reductionist worldview that alienated us from the world outside, but it didn't give us the tools and models to cope with the social, environmental and cultural urgencies of our time and how to act and interact in them. In other words, we don't seem to have the models to engage with the problems of our time because its hard to understand the complex relations, interactions and interdependencies in these social and environmental processes that are embedded in our techno-logical culture and tend to fluctuate between local and global issues.

Over the last 10 years we can see the tendency to establish trans- and interdisciplinary collaborations where knowledge and experience from different domains is mingled to achieve new insights and find new models and directions to deal with contemporary questions and urgencies. One major topic of today's artistic and cultural practice is the interest for interaction as a design issue. It puts forward the question of how interaction between people, machines and objects spontaneously builds strong and weak connections, how networks emerge from that, and how these networks achieve organisation, structure and form, letting diversity and variation emerge.

Understanding and designing interaction in this model is not based on rigid blueprints or detailed plans with clear-cut goals: it proceeds to a large extent messily, in an exploratory and flexible way. Networks - and what they bring about - are emerging bottom-up and not so much top-down.

It is this bottom-up approach, the patching of different know-hows and experiences, and the strong focus on social and cultural interaction, that qualifies The Patching Zone as a unique project. It is an innovative project built on earlier experiments done by Anne Nigten, who directs The Patching Zone. 'Patching the zones' is done bottom-up, thus taking the risk of failure but also the chance of success offering new models for social and cultural innovation and transformation. It is a challenging mission since The Patching Zone is operating within large blue prints of city planners that address social, cultural and economic innovation in certain areas in Rotterdam and other cities in the Netherlands. It means that The Patching Zone has to deal with these agendas in some way or another. Authorities are less interested in the experiment and process in itself, since they want results, solving social and cultural problems within strict time frames. These results are therefore defined within political agendas of policy-makers and might very well interfere with a more sensitive and experimental process, as it is put to work by The Patching Zone, which needs an incubation period and follow up over time. This certainly has an impact on how The Patching Zone can operate, where it can find its space for experiment and its methodology of working, and how it can cope with a more long term agenda needed for the sorts of projects The Patching Zone is developing in for example Rotterdam South.

It is therefore good to see how The Patching Zone is developing over its first two years of activities and how it has organized itself. It maintains maximum flexibility and is indeed able to deliver results within strict time frames. It does so by operating within a rich network of partners in different sectors that not only support the projects by The Patching Zone but are also becoming structural partners that can nurture a project, add value and keep on developing a project in time. The Patching Zone is a typical network organisation that is very much aware of how it contributes to a larger value chain, in which the network partners are essential for the long-term success of a specific project, since they can develop that project

from its experimental stage into a more sustainable stage. This approach guarantees the experimental and innovative approach of The Patching Zone without structuring it too much around the political agenda's it has to deal with.

Based on these observations I'm sure that the social and the cultural Pasta Pesto that The Patching Zone is cooking for us will be tasty and will get better over time.

---

1   Evening of Siegfried Zielinski - The Three Princes of Ser-
     endip i.c.w. David Link, Jan St. Werner (Mouse of Mars)
     en Tomas Fecht - DEAF03.

Introduction

Anne Nigten

The ideas behind the Processpatching approach stem from Processpatching, Defining New Methods in aRt&D, my PhD thesis (2007) that built on my work as manager of the V2_Lab in Rotterdam. Processpatching, defining new methods in aRt&D investigated how electronic art patches together and (re-)mixes processes and methods from the arts, engineering and computer science environments. The investigated collaboration fields I was involved in at that time provided me with case studies and the art-science provided a natural theoretical reference framework for this context. The most pressing outcome of my research at that time was the need for a place where people with different backgrounds could build a shared practice, this lead to the initiation of The Patching Zone (2008). The Patching Zone is a transdisciplinary laboratory for innovation where Master, doctor, post-doc students and young professionals from different backgrounds create meaningful content. In our laboratories the students and researchers work together, supervised by experts, on commissions with creative use of high-tech materials, digital media and / or information technology. The participants come from a range of educational programs such as art schools, design schools, social and computer sciences, technical programs and industry.

The Patching Zone applies the 'Processpatching' approach and has generated over the last two years, input and ideas to develop the processpatching concept further, based on real projects for real people. This lead to some major new insights that The Patching Zone team of supervisors, project participants and myself, would like to share with you. This brings us to another outcome of my PhD study: The desire for practice based theory and the need for a handbook for those who work in this field or who are planning to engage in this collaborative field. So besides informing you about The Patching Zone experience this book revisits some of the basic processpatching ideas and proposes more thorough references based on our experiences so far. In this light the book can be read as a next step for fostering creative collaborative praxis including guidelines and ideas for the near future.

The book is built around the theoretical context of creative transdiscliplinary research and development, the first chapters cover the frequently applied research and development approaches where their elements origins provide references to other fields that are frequently referred to, usually in refreshing and unusual ways. The topics in these chapters are clustered around unconventional creative action research themes. I observed that the processpatching approach has been most fruitful when it moves beyond the text based scientific writing culture, as the team actively uses most of their sensory receptors; vision, hearing, touch and proprioception, taste and smell.

We'll reflect, inform and analyse the effects of these modes of research...

As theory is always informed by practice and visa versa, we'll take you along on our journey to make crossing connections between theory on different levels, such as methodological references, thematic references and practice. The referred practice also covers a multitude of levels and perspectives that includes general findings and detailed observations as well as reflections from the semi-outside world by interviews with the project's stakeholders.

The core section of the book deals with the contributions of our team members who have been invited to contribute in their preferred style or medium. This section includes personal observations and provides insights into the research and development process on many different levels. We have approached people individually although they all have been an important link in the team process, some of the contributors proposed a collaborative contribution that illustrated the pleasure and fun of working together.

The book concludes with the achievements of The Patching Zone so far, the relevance of processpatching and touches the broad ground we have been covering from innovation to social engagement, economic values and artistic qualities. And last but not least we'll outline the challenges for the near future.

We hope you'll enjoy the diversity of resources, opinions and perspectives that mirrors the investigators' and methodological triangulation as one of the key characteristics of processpatching.

Process-patching in context

Anne Nigten

The background-theory of The Patching Zone is rooted in the transdisciplinary collaboration discourse as outlined in 'Transdisciplinarity: recreating integrated knowledge' *(Somerville, M., Rapport, D., 2000)* The transdisciplinary model is different from a multidisciplinary model as it moves beyond the mixing of fields and leads to a new hybrid between the disciplines. This conceptual space between the disciplines is a new field or are new fields, where methods are mixed or given new input, that is beneficial to all disciplines involved. The team members take the relevant parts of the generated knowledge back to their own disciplines. Of course (temporary) migration to other disciplines is possible but not the main objective. This conceptual space between the disciplines could be interpreted as a 'neutral' space, which is not governed by a specific discipline or discourse. *(Nigten, 2008)*

Let's do some time traveling. First, I would like to draw a historic parallel between Process-patching, The Patching Zone's work method, and the Bauhaus education model *(Bayer, Gropius 1938, 1972) (Itten, 1975)*, especially in the relation of the 21st century's notion of practice and 'material' treatment and Bauhaus' craftsmanship. In both occasions there is a direct co-relation between the theory and contextual practice. In both occasions the work is created for direct appliances. Bauhaus' working communities show an interesting resemblance with the collaboration teams and the in situ or embedded students in the local

'We aim to bridge the gap'

context in recent Patching Zone projects. In our 'version' of the work communities, the project teams work together with the stakeholders while living in that specific community. We have come to agreements with the local housing corporations to temporarily accommodate our students and young professionals in the area. The embedded situation brings the barriers between experts and lay people to the surface immediately: street culture expertise, informal wisdom and professional expertise are mingled from day one. We have adapted a bottom-up approach for and with the end-users or participants that fully acknowledges these different layers of expertise.

Of course, also some major differences can be observed between our approaches and Bauhaus. It is widely acknowledged that the Bauhaus teaching model has been very influential for the art and design programmes over the last century where specialism and uniqueness has been, and often still is, the focal point. The Bauhaus was situated in the industrial environment that has changed from a product economy in the glory of the industrial revolution in the early 20th century towards an ex-

perience and service economy of the present day. 'Today, people still buy products mostly for their function; nonmaterialistic reasons remain secondary. But that is changing. In 25 years, what people buy will be mostly stories, legends, emotion, and lifestyle.' *(Jensen, R. 1996)* This evolutionary situation often represents complex issues, as the counterpart of the raise of the digital era and more specifically the introduction of social media. The effects of this are reflected in all kinds of complex issues such as urban regeneration plans, social changes and transitions in people's professional careers. This brings forward new demands regarding the skills and work models for art, design et al.. This requires a mix of disciplinary knowledge and expertise to tackle or engage with the multi layered issues at stake. Here The Patching Zone comes in, as a non-educational programme we aim to bridge the gap between the formal education and research programmes in the field of art, design, technology, science and the professional collaborative practice. One could state that we are bridging the gap between specialists from different programmes and transdisciplinary collaboration by channeling the uniqueness towards multifaceted content production. This devotion to collaboration thus stems from the gap between the specialist education programmes, the complex issues that we are dealing with, and the rich media experiences we are trying to establish. The outlined context above consequently requires a new alliance of disciplines and new strategies. Here I would like to underline that specialists are preferred over generalists. However, the students, researchers and young professionals with a specialist background often lack the knowledge and skills to understand and collaborate with other trained specialists and the stakeholders. We prefer a transdisciplinary collaboration model from a master and pupil model and coach our teams to work outside their comfort zone where new inspiration, experiments and innovation can be established, based on the accumulation of all represented expert knowledge. The Patching Zone is dealing with experiences that are supported by working prototypes rather than market ready products. Furthermore, to finish the analogy with Bauhaus; both Bauhaus and The Patching Zone, have been established in very dynamic time frames where the upcoming changes and unsettling social and economic situation has been (and for The Patching Zone still is) a major challenge and a source of inspiration.

Let's time travel again and jump to the end of the last century : the introduction of the internet and the raise and fall of the dot com business. Here we zoom in on the art and science discourse where our attention is caught by a nuanced shift from the art and technoscience context in the late 20th century (when I started the V2_Lab) and today's co-creation context. At that time the art-science dialogue was revitalized due to the rise of new technology and new media. In this dialogue techno science was prevailing from the creative practice due to its status quo and (research) budgets. *(Nigten, 2007, page 28)* In the contemporary context the focal point has shifted from the techno-scientific towards the end-user or participant. This should be seen in the light of the rise of social media and user driven innovation that followed the technology driven innovation model from the last decades of the 20th century. This also brought along a shift in focal point for the makers; while technoscience was the leading force earlier, today we work with multiple perspectives that connect directly with the human experience factor. We are confronted with the limitations of the dominant 3rd person or objective perspective as promoted by most (techno) scientific branches. With the users' or participants' perspective in the research and development centre, it is required to include a first persons view in the loop. After all personal experiences are by definition subjective. We thus benefit from a multitude of perspectives. Here the artistic and design perspective proves to be useful, as they are educated in an audience or participant oriented way. Ideally one would like to have the option to jump between perspectives during a research and development cycle. The mix of disciplines represented in The Patching Zone team establishes this.

In the following paragraphs I'll present a brief analysis, based on The Patching Zone practices, of the combined views that we applied for experience and participatory design approaches and their related disciplinary background. Media art or electronic art provides interesting subjective (first person's) references in the field of cultural and interactive experience. Over the last decades a breakthrough from technological thinking was established by linking human-computer interaction research to theatre art practice. *(Laurel, 1991)* Meanwhile pioneering electronic artists worked around technological obstacles in a non-technological fashion, often in an intuitive way or with concepts that were based on experience rather than the technological perspective. *(Nigten, 2005, 2007, page 84, 2009)* These artistic experiments have been ever since a source of inspiration into new and open models where interaction softly slides into co-creation. For our work today this explorative open-ended research and development is one of the most relevant lessons learnt from interactive electronic art. It's fascinating to 'read' interactive art by the ways it often gets around the shortcomings and technological obstacles (leaving it to be decided whether this is caused by the technology or by its makers). Electronic art provides us with interesting routines to shift from the shortcomings of the machine towards the participant. After all, the participant deals with emotions and confusion in a split second without complex algorithmic calculations. I would like to underline that this goes further than a smart short-cut, it manifests the knowledge of the makers about complex interaction patterns; how to evoke emotions and seduce the participant into engagement. In essence the interactive artwork here is a framework that includes control switches, so that the participant(s) can take place in the driver's seat if desired.

The participants' experience is the leading objective in the artist ambition. In my earlier writings the importance of uselessness has often been underlined. Here it is crucial to understand that designing for uselessness brings along major research issues: Obviously it is more difficult to design without a task or purpose in mind, simply because one cannot lean on the known goal directed routines and mind-set of the participant. Artistic and design knowledge helps us to design elements that, again, seduce or trigger emotions and (inter)

action. These techniques stem from a range of artistic and design branches, we'll share with you later in this publication. From an engineering and applied point of view these open-ended and thus unpredictable approaches often turn out to be difficult to deal with. The techno scientific and engineers' specialist training today is often based on a problem solving or reductive approach. In several Patching Zone projects we have experienced collisions between the reductive approach that is often applied by engineers and the open-ended artistic approach, this is further complicated by the often unpredictable, stakeholders and co-creators input in the development process. For the creation of meaningful content however, it is crucial to include a larger context while a problem solving approach is often based on a reductive approach. *(Nigten, 2004)* Based on our first experiences we saw that design and engineering find each other in building prototypes for testing and hands-on research and development, or research by making. This has been put in practice in hands-on workshops that resemble, more or less, a series of micro problems to be solved through making it. The value of making as research is another striking outcome of our Patching Zone experiences so far. These workshops also serve another goal; they are organized in all our projects to establish the stakeholders' engagement. Generally spoken, the stakeholders share the preference for concrete (mini) outcomes and we benefit from the current 'creativity' and 'making' trend *(Florida, 2004)*.

The workshop format thus provides an interesting platform for communication among technicians and stakeholders, where feedback and ideas are discussed over the worktable. Here one can state that the materials in these making and doing sessions, work as a boundary object for conversation and exchange as they translate the abstract projects' objectives into a tangible, edible, aural or other concrete temporary outcome. These workshops do not only inform the stakeholders, they also lead to insights and generate new ideas for The Patching Zone teams. For engineers and designers in our teams it combines a pre-defined objective (problem), a clear target while a tunneled topical conversation is also included with lay people. The value of this exchange among engineers and stakeholders is often underestimated; we look at this approach as an important first step towards an inherent dialogue among technicians and co-creators. Besides this the engineers and designers in our teams are always on the lookout for sub problems that are embedded or hidden in the open-ended trajectory. Sometimes this generates impulses for the explorative artistic approach and provides hooks for sub investigations. However, the risk is here that, especially in the starting phase of the project, the objectives and thus the sub problems tend to shift constantly and the developed sub items thus become obsolete or irrelevant. This might be disappointing if one tends to think functionally.

The discussed research and development approaches so far, could all be caught under the collective term 'practice lead' the new alliances as outlined above yield interesting material for social studies and reflective research. The projects realized so far have been incorporated as cases in PhD studies. The life span of our commissions does not, yet, match with a full four-year study trajectory, yet. Another strand we are investigating is a valorisation trajectory for master students from technical universities, where we aim to test and validate prototypes to market. With the hands-on practice lead Processpatching approach, we enable rapid action and work as a catalyst for user driven

'Materials work as a boundary object'

creative R&D and we aim to continue in this direction for longer term projects.

All of our projects have a certain social and creative urgency in common as well as complexity. We prefer to deal with complex issues according to a bottom up approach. From early on in a project we involve the stakeholders. The involvement of our stakeholders adds another layer to the transdisciplinary collaboration amongst the team members. These stakeholders (young people in the Big South Lab project and the Go for IT! project, librarians and archivists in the Cultuur Lokaal project and the population of a deprived street in Recycle-X) play different roles in the phases of the project's development. As outlined in the diagram below the engagement with our stakeholders is divided into short cycles that are set among a general timeline of the project.

Stakeholders engagement
In the initial phase of a project the stakeholders are consulted as guides in our new environment, they act as specialists while The

Production cycle

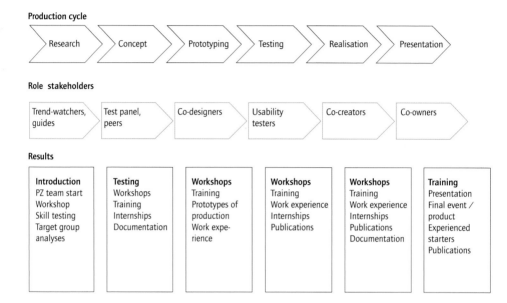

| Research | Concept | Prototyping | Testing | Realisation | Presentation |

Role stakeholders

| Trend-watchers, guides | Test panel, peers | Co-designers | Usability testers | Co-creators | Co-owners |

Results

Introduction	Testing	Workshops	Workshops	Workshops	Training
PZ team start	Workshops	Training	Training	Training	Presentation
Workshop	Training	Prototypes of	Work experience	Work experience	Final event /
Skill testing	Internships	production	Internships	Internships	product
Target group	Documentation	Work expe-	Publications	Publications	Experienced
analyses		rience		Documentation	starters
					Publications

Patching Zone team members observe their new habitat from an outsiders perspective. This intensive form of creative tourism brings cultural differences of all sorts to the surface both to The Patching Zone team and the local guides. In the next phase the stakeholders are invited as experts to review the team's concepts, ideas and observations. From then on the stakeholders roles vary from testers to co-designers, developing over time into co-owners. The proposed cycles are motivated by the stakeholder's interest and attention span, the involvement grows while stakeholders come and go and come back again. These cycles also provide room for our teams to introduce new ideas, techniques and iterations. The time between the indicated phases gives space for reflection, evaluation and iterations of the project among our team members with multiple backgrounds.

Making as Research

Kristina Andersen
and Anne Nigten

As stated in the introduction of this book, theory is always informed by practice and in the case of The Patching Zone, practice is centered around a collaborative process of 'making'. This is a deliberate strategy: We are working with teams that have a large variation in age, cultural background, skill, and methodology. The 'making together' is the process where these backgrounds meet and each participant fall into role, working towards a common goal. In this sense the process can best be described, not as a sewing circle where each member is working on their own craft project in a shared space (parallel play) but rather like a quilting bee, where each member is contributing their hands, eyes, and skills to a communal quilt (project). Quilting bees are also useful references in the sense that one overall design is chosen in an open collaborative process that takes into context the skills and time availability of each collaborating maker. *(Plant, 1997, Nigten, 2007)*

The ongoing challenge for The Patching Zone teams is always the fluid management of these decision and 'making' processes where each participant must feel challenged and inspired when working towards a goal that is aiming to be larger than the sum of it's parts. It is worth clarifying that our 'making as research' process happens on two distinct levels, first within the teams of students and young professionals of The Patching Zone and then between the teams and the local stakeholders in each project. These two levels are intricately

'We are constantly learning how we can achieve convergence of desires'

connected with each other in a recursive flow of opportunities to make and explore ideas in response to, not only the actual physical situations, but also to a mentally and emotionally fluid environment *(Andersen, 2010)*. In this process we are constantly learning how we can achieve convergence of desires and skills rather than bland consensus designs and bricolage. In achieving convergence we must as Anne Galloway (2007) puts it 'take into account and be accountable to things that appear irrelevant or contrary to our personal interest'. In this way we can honour desires and concerns that are not our own, and with along with Anne propose that 'messiness, disjuncture and tension' may not be enemies to collaboration but rather intrinsic qualities of true collaboration.

'Making' relies on full embodied participation, it trancends a mere cognitive process and relies on motorics and time, skills and knowledge. Each participant comes into the process with a specific set of tools and knowlegde 'ready to hand' and the 'making' process is the locus of

the beginning of co-creation. Like other forms of crafts, making your own technology can be seen as a sculptural process of allowing objects to be formed in your hands and as such it is an almost primal process of discovery and recognition. As an object slowly takes form on the table in front of us, we can begin to develop intuitions about its capabilities and behaviour. Maybe in an extreme extrapolation of Hayes' 'naive physics' (1978) we could say that it is through the actual 'making' that we begin to comprehend the objects we are building. *(Andersen, 2007)*

This chapter will outline the main characteristics of 'making' and how it can generate new knowledge and experiences. It will also discuss how an open and collaborative process can be created and supported.

Making knowledge and experiences

In a traditionally delineated field, Art (with and without the capital A) is engaged in the producing of meaningful artefacts and Ethnography is concerned with collecting artefacts in order to document their meaning. When attempting to facilitate a 'make' oriented research, most relevant methods somehow reference both. Cultural Probes and Placebo Design are two examples of art/ethnography crossover methods.

'Cultural Probes' *(Gaver, 1999)* is a method of providing stakeholders with intricately designed opportunities for expression. They may contain cameras with instructions to photograph certain situations or stamped postcards with evocative questions. The probes are not neutral but rather a subjective invitation for an end user to contribute their subjective contribution towards a design. The aim is not only to collect inspirational data, but rather to allow that data to guide the project. These types of methods, while originally considered methodologically subversive, have become very widely used in mainstream user-centered technology design *(Boehner, et al., 2007)*. 'Design Placebos', like medical placebos, are designs that do not actually solve any problem. Instead they are created to simply address an underlying concern or issue and potentially shift the way that people think about a situation. Rather than altering reality in any scientifically tangible way, they provide psychological comfort as people develop narratives that explain how their world is different as a direct result of what the placebo is imagined to be doing. Design placebos must be open ended enough to prompt stories, but not so open as to bewilder *(Dunne & Raby, 2002)*.

The aim in both of these aproaches is to encourage a Coleridge-esque willing suspension of disbelief and to engage people in the active re-imagination of the world. Bennett (2001) describes enchantment as being 'both caught up and carried away'. According to McCarthy (2006) "when it comes to experiences such as enchantment feelings are as important as thoughts, sensation is as important as cognition, and emotional consciousness is as important as will". Enchantment engages directly with paradox and ambiguity, and ambiguity in turn leaves space for meaning-making. Gaver et al. (2003) writes at length about allowing ambiguity as a resource for design and in that sense it can be said that these methods take

their origin in quite traditional art context. Only it is an art context, that has been opened for participation and the resulting artefacts are collected and treated in ways that reference ethnography. And it is an ethnography, where the collected material has been prompted and produced in a deliberate effort. Of course Art is in it's essence collaborative, it is as much a social as it is an intellectual or practical discipline. It requires all of those elements to work *(Esche, 2007)* and at the same time "ethnography is not only 'about' the culture under study, but equally, implicitly or explicitly, 'about' the cultural perspective from which it is written and that of the audience to whom

'Culture -the object of anthropological ethnographic inquiry- as stories'

it is presented. Clifford Geertz famously described culture – the object of anthropological ethnographic inquiry – as "stories that people tell themselves about themselves," and, by the same token, by telling an ethnographic story about some Other, the ethnographer also tells a story about ourselves." *(Dourish, 2006)*

These two methods are especially interesting to us, simply because they are centered around a dual process of 'making'. The probes and placebos are designed and made with a deliberately porous core that allows another, later making process to take place within and around them, when they are deployed to their end-users. This means that they closely resemble The Patching Zone projects, where the teams make structures and proposals for experiences that allow and prompt shareholders to co-create with us and with each other. For us then, the ethnographic moment is present throughout, the knowledge generated is as likely to be found in a fleeting street conversation as a well executed object, that can be

''Making', for both thinking out loud and thinking together'

photographed and documented. Amongst the artefacts and the traces; our focus lies as much in paying attention to our own hands and their hands, as it does in the 'making' itself.

Paying attention

A constant challenge for any Patching Zone project is to pay careful attention to the process itself as we move across methodologies and situations. The phrase 'to pay attention' gives an insight into itself: the attention must be 'paid', it is a resource spent and used. This is not lightly done, it requires a sober commitment to listening to and noting the rumblings of the systems we are enmeshing ourselves into. In a fashion reminisent of Big Tent strategies, we span diverse groups, both within the project itself and the stakeholders we work with. Each of these groups may have very different agendas and criterias for success, but they come together in short time frames to focus on the thing at hand: the object of collaborative creation.

'Making', as a method for both thinking out loud and thinking together, is a process that

functions to establishing common ground. Dourish (2001) describes common ground as 'a set of commonly held and mutually established facts that provide the background necessary for interpreting and understanding utterances.' These facts can include a sharing of skills and falling into roles, a mutual understanding of the issues at hand and the rules of the engagement, etc.. Once this ground is established we can proceed with 'making' together in a workshop format or a public intervention format. By paying attention to these events, we allow for analysis and meaning being ascertained 'after the fact', sometimes harnessing knowledge, but always engaging each other in questioning what we do and how we do it. David Garcia (2007) draws our attention to the mirror space; as uncommon ground, where a "creative enstrangement from the assumptons that underpins the usual networks and rituals" allows us to explicitly pay attention to the process and through what is basically a form of structural deliberate misunderstanding, allow for the unexpected idea, the innovation.

This process is sympathetic to the educational games of Froebel's Kindergarden where the systematic deployment of objects with associated activities is aimed squarely nurturing creativity and paying attention to the 'how' rather than the 'what'. 'Kindergarten sewing was to sewing as kindergarten drawing was to drawing - the emphasis in each was not on the thing rendered but on the elements of the work' (Brosterman, 1997). Keeping in mind that enchantment is not even imaginable without the acute sensory activity that notices the sensuousness of every thing *(McCarthy, et al., 2006)*. Dr. Montessori of course famously used blindfolds in reviewing materials, stating that the eye can interfere with what the hand knows *(Lillard, 2005)*.

Our emphasis is on empowering both the teams and the stakeholders to take ownership of not only their own situation and process but also the technology they employ. "Making that excitement and its conceptualisation express-ible in both descriptive, sensual and technical terms that leaves the small marks readable and usable by others through all stages of the work is key for design work that develops in dialogue across teams" *(Andersen, Fuller, Nigten, 2005)*. We are making our home-made technological objects to the best of our collective ability and the limitations we face are our own. This is a way for each participant to retain some level of control over both the work, and the process through which it is be-ing made.

Supporting an open making process and playing along

The question of how we can work together manifests itself in the more practical; how can we 'make' together? It is useful to keep in mind that 'making' can also be said to be a form of play as long as one keeps in mind that playing is not necessarily light-hearted or fun; but rather a way of approaching a particular design space and a set of rules and limitations *(Caillois, 1961)*. I would like to propose that when we set out to establish, how we go about creating the circumstances for successful col-

laborative making, we can look at playing and circumstances that support playfulness.

Caillois (1961) describes playing as a move to another reality, where the rules of the real world are replaced with precise and essential rules that the person playing must adapt to. In order to play, one must accept the rules of the game and this acceptance must be voluntary and free, as freedom and choice are charac-teristics of play itself. The narrative framework of a game enables players to accept rules and constraints that deviate from their everyday life whilst maintaining a feeling of freedom and spontaneity. This is supported by the

'Empowering both the teams and the stakeholders'

fact that the game occurs within a time and space constraint that is identified and set be-forehand. It is temporary and we enter into it knowing that it will end and we will be able to take back our everyday life, when the game is over. *(Andersen, et al., 2004)*

In a similar way, a Patching Zone project comes with a explicit set of deliverables and rules. It is set in a locale (for example Gouda) and within a situation (the archive, the library and the museum). It comes with a predefined set of stakeholders and a fixed time frame. The participants are choosing to relocate to this other reality for the project duration and are as such very aware of the disruption of their ordinary lives. The stakeholders are invited to enter into collaboration on an 'event by event' basis. These events often take the form of interventions or workshops, more details about the specific events can be found in the contributions from the participants in Go for IT!, Big South Lab and Recycle-X.

Two other key concepts in play are immersion and involvement. Games have the power to prompt someone's real cognitive and emotional participation. Csikszentmihalyi (1990) uses playing as an example of the highly energized and enjoyable state of concentration and focus that he defines as 'flow'. This means that by entering play-mode a person is able to fully engage, while at the same time having a strong experience. This implies that playfulness can be used to trigger more emotional participation from users than more traditional participatory methods. This of course works both ways, strong immersion and involvement can lead to strong emotional experiences of all kinds.

When it comes to engaging our stakeholders, playfulness can also be a way of supporting expression and creativity. As surrealist and situationist artists discovered, games can provide an alternative reality that allows people to let down their guard, access the unconscious, and cross boundaries they might not have otherwise crossed. Through playful procedures and methodologies of the fantastic, surrealist games lead to 'out of the ordinary' situations where the player is allowed to express her or himself in a spontaneous and emotionally genuinely way *(Gooding, 1995)*. We will detail our take on audience participation in the following chapters.

Conclusions

'Making' allows us to direct our attention both inwards to our teams and outwards to our stakeholders as we play and probe our way through the situations at hand. It is an ongoing process of discovery and failure. We use our limited abilities to create something that did not exist before: unusual behaviours, objects that exist in response to situations and places and people. Along the way we sometimes expose unexpected and poetic possibilities that can be explored from our specific vantage point: new materials, economies or contexts that create and support paradox, openness, ambiguity and the transformational character of experience. The joy of making things together is the driver behind our work, it is this engaging with the matter at hand that provides the reward and the trigger for our ongoing experiments in how we can meet each other. This is only possible when we pay attention and carefully allow for openess, trust, flow and remember to keep our eye on the ball.

It is like anything else, you have to start somewhere: 'If you are new to walking, begin with the familiar. Make short but useful trips, with clear goals and ways to measure achievement. Use walking instrumentally; in this way, it will no longer feel like an anomaly in your life.' *(Pope, 2000)*

References:

Andersen, K., Developing your own hardware, In: Digital Artists' Handbook, www.digitalartistshandbook.org/hardware, 2007

Andersen, K., Fuller, M., Nigten, A., '~worn~', In: Proc. Wearable Futures - Hybrid Culture in the Design and Development of Soft Technology, University of Wales, 2005

Andersen, K., Intuition, IN: Proc. Music and Machines X:Resistant Materials II, Newcastle University, 2010

Andersen, K., Jacobs, M., Polazzi, L., IF ONLY: bringing dreams into practice, In: Proc. 4th International Conference on Design and Emotion, Ankara, 2004

Bennett, J., The Enchantment of Modern Life: Attachments, Crossings, Princeton: Princeton University Press, 2001

Boehner, K., Vertesi, J., Sengers, P., Dourish, P., How HCI Interprets the Probes, In Proc. CHI 2007, New York: ACM Press, 2007

Brosterman, N., Inventing Kindergarten, Harry N. Abrams, 1997

Caillois, R., Man, Play, Games, Illinois: University of Illinois Press, 1961

Csikszentmihalyi, M., Flow: The psychology of optimal experience, New York: Harper & Row, 1990

Dourish, P., Being-in-the-World: Embodied Interaction, In: Where the Action is: The Foundations of Embodied Interaction, Cambridge: MIT Press, 2001

Dourish, P., Implications for Design, In: Proc. CHI 2006, New York: ACM Press, 2006

Dunne, A., Raby, F., The Placebo Project, In: Proc. DIS 2002, New York: ACM Press, 2002

Esche, C., How to grow Possibility:the Potential Roles of Academies, In: AIR# Let's suppose the Academy is a place for artists... , Amsterdam: Amsterdam school of the Arts, 2007

Garcia, D., Introduction, In (Un)common Ground: Creative Encounters across Sectors and Disciplines, A'dam: BIS Publishers, 2007

Galloway, A., Seams and Scars, Or How to Locate Accountability in Collaborative Work, In (Un)common Ground: Creative Encounters across Sectors and Disciplines, A'dam: BIS Publishers, 2007

Gaver, W., Beaver, J., and Benford, S., Ambiguity as a Resource for Design, In: Proc. CHI 2003, New York: ACM Press, 2003

Gaver, W., Dunne, T., and Pacenti, E., Cultural Probes, IN: Proc. CHI 1990, New York: ACM Press, 1999

Gooding, M., (Ed.), A Book of Surrealist Games, Boston, MA: Shambhala Redstone Editions, 1995

Hayes, P., The naive physics manifesto, In: Systems in the Micro-Electronic Age, Edinburgh: Edinburgh University Press, 1978

Lillard, A.S., Montessori: The Science Behind the Genius,, Oxford: Oxford University Press, 2005

McCarthy, J., Wright, P., Wallace, J., Dearden, A., The Experience of Enchantment in Human–Computer Interaction, In: Proc. Personal and Ubiquitous Computing 10, New York: ACM Press, 2006

Plant, S., Zeros + Ones: Digital Women and the New Technoculture, London: Fourth Estate, 1997

Pope, S., Starting, In London Walking, a Handbook for Survival, London: Batsford Ltd, 2000

Playing as Research

Kristina Andersen, Sam Nemeth and Anne Nigten

Playing is an important aspect in the lives of both children and adults. It is in play that we are able to process and imagine change within our everyday worlds. Playing will not immediately change any of the external realities of our situations but it is a vehicle for exploring the negative and positive aspects of our lives and for a brief time create an alternate space in which we might imagine new and different experiences. Winnicott (1971) states that it is "in playing, and only in playing, that the individual child or adult is able to be creative and to use the whole personality, and it is only in being creative that the individual discovers

the self". This is of course in some ways old news, Plato is reported to have observed "you can discover more about a person in an hour of play than in a year of conversation".

A 'typical' Patching Zone project generally has a number of properties that make a playful approach almost unavoidable. In this chapter we elaborate on several applications of playing as research and it's relation to gaming. Within our projects playing is often used as a fun way to explore the work environment and as an introduction of the team to the audience or target group. As stated earlier this can be an informal way to get to unwritten information about the stakeholders, the atmosphere and spirit of the areas where our projects are situated. In playful approaches one often observes an openness and willingness to engage that is of crucial importance to audience involvement. Using playfulness to introduce a site and a situation: Fun and enjoyment are spontaneous aspects of human life, they are difficult to isolate, observe or measure. However, they can be provoked and facilitated. Like storytelling and poetry, playfulness and games are valuable instruments that can trigger sincere responses within artificial situations. These situations or games can then become frameworks for exploring and experiencing the issues at hand and we can use them to take a fresh view of the complex situations we work within.

So what do we mean by playing? One way of explaining it, is that play is an approach to action, not a form of activity. In other words, the subject and style of play is unimportant, it is the manner in which you approach something that makes an exercise playful. This means that we can be playful about serious matters as long as our way of addressing an issue follows the rules of play.

Caillois (1961) describes playing as a move to another reality, where the rules of the real world are replaced with precise and essential rules that the person playing must adapt to. In order to play, one must accept the rules of the game and this acceptance must be voluntary and free, as freedom and choice are characteristics of play itself. The narrative framework of a game enables players to accept rules and constraints that deviate from their everyday life whilst maintaining a feeling of freedom and spontaneity. This is supported by the fact that the game occurs within a time and space constraint that is identified and set beforehand. It is temporary and we enter into it knowing that it will end and we will be able to take back our everyday life, when the game is over. *(Andersen, et al., 2004)*

'Reality' is a multifaceted term in all our projects, the team members come from all over the planet and end up in a new, mostly unknown, reality such as the picturesque Gouda, a deprived part of Rotterdam or a desolated street in Dordrecht while our stakeholders are drawn in the mediated realities by a highly educated team. These are basic ingredients for everyone involved to move into an imaginative Patching Zone reality.

Two other key concepts in play are immersion and involvement. Games have the power to prompt someone's real cognitive and emotional participation. Csikszentmihalyi (1990) uses playing as an example of the highly energised and enjoyable state of concentration and focus that he defines as 'flow'. This means that by entering play-mode a person is able to fully engage, while at the same time having a strong experience. This implies that playfulness can be used to trigger more emotional participation from users than more traditional participatory methods. This of course works both ways; strong immersion and involvement can lead to strong emotional experiences of all kinds.

When it comes to engaging our stakeholders, playfulness can also be a way of supporting expression and creativity. As surrealist and situationist artists discovered, games can provide an alternative reality that allows people to let down their guard, access the unconscious, and cross boundaries they might not have otherwise crossed. Through playful procedures and methodologies of the fantastic, surrealist games lead to 'out of the ordinary' situations where the player is allowed to express her or himself in a spontaneous and emotionally genuinely way *(Gooding, 1995)*.

It is useful to keep in mind that 'making' can also be said to be a form of play as long as one keeps in mind that playing is not necessarily light-hearted or fun; but rather a way of approaching a particular design space and a set of rules and limitations *(Caillois, 1961)*. Bennet in turn describes how for children "play acts as an integrating mechanism which enables children to draw on past experiences, represent them in different ways, make connections, explore possibilities, and create a sense of meaning" (1996). When we set out to describe how we can support successful collaborative making, it is useful to keep in mind play and circumstances that support playfulness.

We should distinguish gaming from playing. Wittgenstein (1953) points out that there is no common nature of games. Some but not all games are amusing or involve competition but there is only a network of 'overlapping and criss-crossing' similarities between games, not a common feature running through all games. Playing becomes a game when exploratory unstructured playing solidifies into a set of rules often connected through some sort of

narrative framework or goal. Those playing the game must temporarily accept that alternative reality and it's precise and essential rules. The time and space constraints Caillois identifies remain important in order to provoke immersion and make believe. Games are in our context understood as detached from their current

'We should distinguish gaming from playing'

popular meanings through competition driven video games or Role Playing Games. Instead we see games as a way to understand design and to use elements of playfulness to make social design more attractive and effective. Playing games then becomes a more general term that is not necessarily associated with material interest *(Huizinga, 1950/1971)*. In our games we focus instead on concepts of terms of playfulness, social interaction, exploration, make believe and fun. The boundaries set by game rules create a common ground that connects players from different cultures, disciplines and backgrounds. It also foregrounds implicit cultural differences, that could lead to new or other insights and of course, confusion or misunderstandings among the participants.

In many of the workshops with our young target groups the traditional competitive aspect of gaming is the initial driving force for their engagement, it seems to resonate with popular youth culture and mass-media formats that are mostly based on competitive forms. We then play with the concept of competing and winning by bending the game more towards playfulness. For example, one of the rules set by the team for the Go for IT! project, was that we would not introduce prizes or awards. Here we challenged the most common materialistic street code: What is in it for me? Instead we choose to highlight the winner's reputation and status as an attractive and desirable outcome. By eliminating a traditional point based reward system we have more freedom to reward various kinds of positive behaviors within the game. Through rewarding social interaction and team play we try to move the games from competition towards collaboration.

In many of The Patching Zone projects our first objective is to connect people and to stimulate

'We challenged the most common materialistic street code'

them to interact with each other. Here a collaborative game structure is very helpful. Playing, as a trigger to make-belief and fun can also guide and facilitate innovation of ideas and experiences. There is a long tradition for this type of thinking. In 1950 Huizinga describes culture itself as "arising in the form of play, that it is played from the very beginning". Winnicott (1971) states: "The place where cultural experience is located is in the potential space between the individual and the environment (originally the object). The same can be said of playing. Cultural experience begins with creative living first manifested as play" and Carl Jung declared that the "creation of something new is not accomplished by the intellect but by the play instinct acting from inner necessity" (1971).

Before we started work on the Cultuur Lokaal project in Gouda, we had been told stories of complicated local networks and social situations within the city that appeared to be at a stale mate. When we arrived we saw beautiful quaint cityscapes and a lively trade and shop culture. What was the real story? Our team was very international, coming from as far afield as Brazil and Australia. How were we to introduce the city while separating reality from prejudice? Our very first move was to 'get lost'. The art of getting lost is an old and tried artistic technique, first described by Walter Benjamin in 'the Flâneur' (1999) and later used by both the surrealists and situationists *(Coverley, 2006)*. It requires an initial playful setup and a set of rules to govern the movement through a city. The aim is to allow the game system to guide you in such a way that you will become estranged to the spaces around you, allowing you to experience them in an open and new fashion.

The game we played that first day was simple: the group was divided into couples, and each couple was given a 'getting lost device' and an old fashioned compass. The 'device' was a variation of an old childhood classic, the fortune teller or cootie catcher[1] is a folded paper game where one player holds the device and the other through two series of unguided choices (pick a number, pick a colour) arrives at a 'random' answer or instruction. In this case the instruction was to walk in a particular direction

1   seacoast.sunderland.ac.uk/~asObgr/coot/about.htm

(north, south etc) until your path is obstructed and then use the device again. This version of the device was inspired by Simon Pope in the book 'London Walking' (2000). The teams were also equipped with a map to help them find their way back when the experience was over and they were finding themselves thoroughly lost. The teams all returned eventually to our workspace and told each other how they had experienced the city as they walked. These insights where the basis for short interventions done the following day.

This type of playful games demand what Coleridge called a 'suspension of disbelief' (1817) and it is our experience that when participants are immersed in these kind of experiences, they are generally willing to accept the internal logic of the experience, even though this logic deviates from the logic of the real world. Murray (1998) goes further and suggests that creators of games need to not only suspend disbelief but 'actively create belief' by allowing players to manipulate objects and engage in enactment rather than processing descriptions. The types of games that we engage in should not be 'executed' as much as 'lived'. This is a helpful notion in situations where you are using playfulness and games as a way to imagine solutions and alternatives to uncomfortable realities.

In the Rotterdam South urban transformation area (Go for IT! and Big South Lab) we set up several video workshops for the local community with playful goals: One of the assignment was: Go to a location and tell somebody else's story, connect different video to separately recorded audio. Such an assemblage of course leads to hilarious results and this small experiment lead to the creation of an entire website of stories on video. The workshops are driven by a system of facilitating the local youth to teach each other, inspired by Boal's 'theatre of the oppressed' (1993). Our stakeholders diagram *(see page 16)* includes a blend of role changing patterns that are known from social media and web 2.0 applications, with ideas that can be traced back to simultaneous dramaturgy. In our model the swapping of authority roles between teacher and student and peer teaching as a model for co-creation carries strong links to the swapping of roles between actor and audience. The empowerment of our participants is, after all, key for the sustainability and the long-term impact of our projects. It is this transfer of authority that facilitates the real long term co-ownership of the projects.

When introducing fun as drivers in our projects, it is important for us to use a type of play that has its roots in the culture of the target group and stakeholders. We build our applications in close co-operation and collaboration with the eventual users of an application. By building on the playfulness that is already there in potential, either consciously or sub consciously, we have a playful way to offer technology to a target group that might otherwise be deterred by the complexity and the learning curve. As an example the Go for IT! game system evolved through workshops where playing and gaming were the central topics. We found that emerging computer games with a strong physical component like Dance Dance Revolution were especially appreciated by the youth and this, together with the very strong local sports tradition, lead the team to be used as starting points for designed prototype games. These games were then in turn played on the local sport days and the basketball players that inspired the system in the first place confirmed their reputation: the best dribblers in the hood. With each prototype played on and with, we could let the system evolve in a direction and at a pace that suited our stakeholders, the local youth.

The last reference to playing we would like to highlight here doesn't refer to gaming but to playing as a band; making music as a team with loose rules or etiquettes as in jazz jamming sessions as outlined by Howard Becker *(Becker 2000)*. There is a clear parallel between a jazz band, that is a group of multiple indivual talents who play as an organised team and The Patching Zone teams. All work in a structured way, with respect for one anothers specialism and with room for improvisation and a solo here and there. A comparable format for playing can be observed in many of the workshops and test sessions such as the 'Plantas Parlentas' installation in the Recycle-X project. Where the team turned itself (literally) into a band to give a live concert with the talking plants as their instruments. While the participants enjoyed themselves afterwards with making sounds through plants, water, a simple electronic circuit and their body as if they were part of the rehearsal session.

McCarthy et al states that "to acknowledge that it is important enough to create an environment where personally significant aspects of a person's life can be referenced and paid attention to is to engage with and respect the concerns and hopes of another person" (2005). We try to facilitate environments that are not filled by us with readymade content and narratives, but rather allows our local collaborators to pay attention to and address themselves in relation to each other and the community they are in. This deep-rooted respect for the lives and experiences of the people we work with lies at the core of our playfulness. Fun is intrinsically voluntary and participatory and we believe it is a productive method to engage with the 'whole' of the difficult situations we find ourselves in. Our games are not to be passively experienced or consumed but are scaffolds to facilitating new embodied experiences. Additionally it is our experience that a playful approach adds to both the attractiveness to participating in the work process and the intrinsic value of an application. It makes for richer and more appropriate result, created with and for the stakeholders in environments where fun and games are a serious concern.

References:

Andersen, K., Jacobs, M., Polazzi, L., IF ONLY: bringing dreams into practice, In: Proc. 4th International Conference on Design and Emotion, Ankara, 2004

Andersen, K., Jacobs, M., and Polazzi, L, Playing games in the emotional space, In M. Blythe, A. Monk, C. Overbeeke and P.C. Wright. (Eds.), Funology: From Usability to User Enjoyment, Kluwer, Dordrecht, 2003

Benjamin, W., The Arcades Project, Belknap/Harvard University Press, 1999

Bennet, N., Wood, L. and Rogers, S., Teaching through play: teachers' theory and classroom practice, Buckingham: Open University Press, 1996

Boal, A., Theater of the Oppressed, New York:Theatre Communications Group, 1993

Caillois, R., Man, Play, Games, (M Barash, Trans.), Champaign: University of Illionois Press, 1961

Coleridge, S. T., Biographia Literaria; or Biographical Sketches of my Literary Life and Opinions, London: Rest Fenner, 1817

Coverley, M., Psychogeography, London: Pocket Essentials, 2006

Csikszentmihalyi, M., Flow: The psychology of optimal experience, New York: Harper & Row, 1990

Gooding, M., Ed., A Book of Surrealist Games, Boston, MA: Shambhala Redstone Editions, 1995

Huizinga, J., (originally published in 1938), Homo Ludens: A Study of the Play Element in Culture, Beacon Press, Boston, 1955

Jung, C., C.G. Jung: Psychological Reflections: A New Anthology of His Writings 1905-1961, Jolande Jacobi (ed.), London: Routledge, 1971

McCarthy, J., Wright, P., Wallace, J., and Dearden, A., The experience of enchantment in human-computer interaction, Personal and Ubiquitous Computing Volume 10(6), Springer-Verlag, London, 2005

Murray, J., Hamlet on the Holodeck, Cambridge, MA: MIT Press, 1998

Nigten, A., Jones, S., Play in IEEE Multimedia, November issue, 2006

Pope, S., London Walking, Ellipsis/Batsford Architecture, 2000

Sofer, A., The Stage Life of Props, Ann Arbor: The University of Michigan Press, 2003

Winnicott, D. W., Playing: Its theoretical status in the clinical situation, In Therapeutic Consultations in Child Psychiatry, London: Hogarth Press, 1971

Wittgenstein, L., Philosophical Investigations, Blackwell, Oxford 1953

Becker, H, The Etiquette of Improvisation' in 'Mind, Culture, and Activity', v. 7(3), 171-176.) home.earthlink.net/~hsbecker/, 2000

Participation and co-creation

Anne Nigten

The complexity of the issues that most of The Patching Zone projects are dealing with, benefit from an open approach. Participation that could lead to co-ownership turns out to be a crucial ingredient for sustainable effects of our projects. In order to achieve this, we try to define our projects at the start as open ended. Of course we respect our commissioners' wish list and the desired deliverables. However, it is of great importance to negotiate, with our commissioner or funders, a certain space for innovation or for the unexpected that allows input from our team members and the people formerly known as audience or end-users. The

Patching Zone teams often act as catalyst to set in motion new processes that should be continued and further developed by the stakeholders, whether these are professionals in the cultural or social field, business professionals or street kids, they all need to make these processes their own, engage with it and identify themselves with the outcomes. Most projects we developed so far are part of a problem in a larger context, including aspects and forces that are beyond our control. This demands a certain kind of flexibility and at least an awareness of growth in unpredictable directions. For this reason we can not and do not

'Specific tastes, spices and flavours connected people'

want to work with innovative outcomes that are set in stone prior to the start of the project. Instead we prefer to work with open scenarios that can be further developed by the stakeholders, after our completion of the project. In this chapter we'll visit some of the most occurring references that support this process of audience participation and co-creation and continue with the practical models we developed to implement this in our practice.

Affiliations with concepts from other fields

Boundary objects
Boundary objects are probably the most frequently used concept borrowed from social studies, in a project such as Cultuur Lokaal the team often used principles such as those outlined by Susan L. Star *(Star et all, 1990)*. The boundary object serves as a placeholder or a concept for exchange and communication where all involved participants can relate to. In 'Forgotten Food', one of the Cultuur Lokaal interventions where 16th and 17th century recipes were cooked and served by the cultural heritage archivists at the market place, food served as a boundary object between the market shoppers, our team, the street musicians and the archivists. Communication through food is a well-know feature, however, we also witnessed that the specific tastes, spices and flavours connected people from different cultures, as spices that were brought in by the

Dutch colonialists at that time, also took other routes that lead to the contemporary Mediterranean kitchen, that is most familiar to the migrant families in Gouda. The served food functioned as a boundary object for exchange; the visitors left their own recipe, it thus also served as placeholder for conversation while eating and thinking about the ingredients of ones own recipe the first steps towards community building was established. In Recycle-X our team frequently worked with food and ecologically grown vegetables as boundary objects as well. The Recycle-X team organized brunches and diners as informal meeting events for the street's inhabitants and entrepreneurs. In the 'Slow-Wagon' street performance the Recycle-X team, dressed up as chefs, attracted the audience in the street with free, ecologically grown local vegetables and fruit, these were the boundary objects to start a conversation about ecological initiatives in Dordrecht, where the project was situated. After the conversation they gave out a diary-like booklet with interviews they had made with local ecological activists and key-persons. Also in other Recycle-X events, the tools or the material worked as a boundary object, for example in the Recycle-X workshop 'Talking with Plants' people were invited to make circuits to generate sounds from the plant's soil. The plants worked as a boundary object to interact with the plants and with one another.

In the Go for IT! workshops, The Patching Zone team gathered end user's information such as game preferences and skills, the conceptual space for information exchange also mirrors temporary space as a kind of 'game-space' that allows for spontaneous transactional re-

34

lationships between collaborating performers. This ties together the ethnographic model as outlined by Star with open ended or process focused artistic work, where improvisation is applied to inhibit the negotiation spaces. In several projects our teams experienced this game-space or space for negotiation as a feature and as an obstacle. If one really needs input from the end-user or the stakeholder this space to play can sometimes take too long and it is hard to gain useful input in time to fit your production plans.

Action Research

According to a truly holistic processspatching approach we copy, adjust and re-interpret useful approaches from other knowledge fields such as social sciences, here action research is among the favourites. Action research, once introduced by Kurt Lewin *(Lewin, 1946)* is usually referred as a reflective process of progressive problem solving that aims to improve strategies or solutions for practical issues. This is an interesting link that informs us about ways to work with reflection and observation as part of the iterative process of making and doing (see 'Making as research'). It implies the embedded position of our team members; they are becoming part of the community by observing, doing and co-creating. This brings us to the last variant I would like to bring forward before moving to other reference fields, anthropology; especially when combined with design research. Design anthropology offers us interesting insights. It is known that polls or questionnaires have their limitations, especially in areas that have been overwhelmed with questionnaires for decades and where often problems (as an outcome of the these ques-

tionnaires) equal money for those who carry out the questionnaires. This explains why we experienced certain questionnaire tiredness in specific neighborhoods in Rotterdam South. The interesting aspect of design anthropology is that it uses some of the observation techniques that are similar to action research with the intention to improve people's interaction with their (daily) environment or as some claim in short; it aims to improve human life, although our goals are modest compared to the latter ambition but it explains our interest in the embedded and pro-active attitude that we promote to our team members. Finally the workshops and hands-on experiences, as outlined earlier, also provide us with information about the participant's interests in a very informal way that is similar to action research approaches.

Design and art

Design and art are of great importance for us as a practice of doing and making (see also the references in the previous chapters) here I would like to highlight some of these that relate especially to participation and co-creation. Community arts is among one of these, in the 1970's this was a flourishing practice although in retrospect the working model usually referred to art in a rather instrumental way while in today's area of social media and interactive applications this model is re-shaped towards a negotiation model as outlined by Declan McGonacle *(Buttler and Reiss eds, 2009)*. This model of negotiation sounds familiar to us, as mentioned earlier, giving, taking and sharing are of major importance for successful co-creation in most Patching Zone projects. This bottom up approach acknowledges different roles and different fields of expertise that show us that the notions of professionals and amateurs can turn around during the process. For example in the Big South Lab project the youngsters from the street brought in valuable street knowledge while our team members share their design skills and a multitude of local rap genres are brought in, in exchange for software and design skills. These are brought together in the co-creation process. Again here I would like to underline the importance of an openended approach, as these emerging genres are not predictable from the drawing table prior to the start of the project.

Other important lessons on co-creation can be learnt from media art works that provide a framework for interaction, in earlier writings I referred to other movements in performance art by Marina Abramoviç and Ulay and Fluxus *(Nigten, 2007)*. Such frameworks can be found in several Patching Zone projects, such as the Go for IT! city game; in its current prototype version with interactive street tiles, the games one can play on the tiles are based on a pre-defined rule set that should be activated by a mobile phone call to a toll-free number. Here the tiles and the game rules are the framework for interaction and facilitate both the individual experience and the social interaction simultaneously and in real-time. However, the youth's daily playing on the street reality, brought new insights to the surface. These days we see young kids, younger than our initial target group, dancing their improvised games with multiple players or on their own. They found out that without the telephony component and without the score registration the Go for IT! framework offered plenty of opportunities for their person-alised game scenarios. The VJacket, a jacket developed by the Big South Lab team that is equipped with multiple sensors to modify images and sound, is another example of such an open framework for playful interaction. The user-scenario and interaction model of the VJacket is entirely based on the user/creator's creativity; the VJacket is the interface that enables the user, to interpret their personal movements, pace visually and/or sonically by their personal preferences. At the moment of writing the team carries out experiments with local talented dancers, to test the sensor placements and also the fashion trends for different target groups are investigated.

In Cultuur Lokaal, the pre-designed map of the city on a mobile studio offered this framework for participants to mark their favorite or most important spot with spray-paint. In Go for IT! the pre-selected technology in a QR spy game provided this framework, where participants could design the content (and the story) for their own game and so on. In all these occasions the outcomes are in the hands of the participants. Here an expert–layperson co-creation process is set in motion.

These interactive 'make and do' environments orchestrate fluid interaction and co-creation processes amongst the participants who often do not know each other. These pieces have built–in parameters for (unspoken) negotiation for a shared experience. The above-mentioned experiments are a source of inspiration into new and more open models of interaction. Moreover, user driven interaction offers us exciting routines to de-route the shortcomings of the machine towards the participant. After all, the participant knows how to deal with emotions, irony, confusion and seduction without complex algorithms in a split second. This goes beyond a smart shortcut, it manifests the knowledge of the makers about arousal, how to evoke emotions and seduce the participant into engagement and co-creation. What we can learn from interactive works as open frameworks for interaction; is that the provided space for personal explorations and social interactions are crucial to establish one's personal, deep or immersive media experience. This is an important addition to the theory as outlined by Marc van Doorn and Arjen De Vries *(Doorn, van Vries, de 2006)* who refer to experiences that are formed from a subject-oriented approach by drawing a parallel to performance and life as a social theatre. The above examples outline the multifaceted role of the participant; as conductor within a specific repertoire, the immersive engine story, the main actor and audience. All of this builds on the desire or interest for individual approaches and personal experiences.

Third Space

Participatory design is the last field I would like to address for this informative journey. Although this field has its origins in a very different field, the Scandinavian workplace democratization, it brought forward relevant concepts for our practice such as the Third Space in Human Computer Interaction. *(Muller, 2002)* In our projects we often choose between the Third Space concept and the earlier mentioned, boundary object principle. Muller introduces us to the idea of a concep-

tual third space as an in-between domain, as uncommon ground, as a conceptual space for negotiation, for sharing ideas that cannot be claimed by one (dominating) discipline or expert field. Earlier I referred to this as a neutral space, a space where not everyone involved is familiar with, here new ideas can often come into existence due to the absence of disciplinary boundaries or pre-determined expertise territories. These areas often function as a fertile space for remixing and co-creation experiments *(Nigten, 2007)*.

The concepts of the Third Space can be found back in the workshops, where the making of things creates a new conceptual space where

'A conceptual space for
negotiation,
for sharing ideas'

people work outside their usual or daily environment. It's fun and nice to make something, to create something one usually wouldn't think of. These workshops are experiences where people make things together, the participants and the 'workshop leaders' create a personal journey. Of course the workshops generate a certain kind of empowerment as known from the DIY culture.

Playing is another way to engage with the audience and get them actively involved in the process. Several game-playing genres and playing as a non-competitive performative act create spaces for shared experiences. Especially unknown games or improvisations, again a reference to the boundary object or third space evens out the obstacle to interact with unknown or unfamiliar other players.

Model

The diagram *(see page 16)* shows, based on our work so far, how the stakeholder's role evolves from an initial guide, to co-designer and finally transforms into the co-owner. A most commonly known (traditional) production cycle is used as a baseline to illustrate the participant's role through out the project's development.

The availability over time is an issue we are often confronted with, the stakeholders often have limited time or interest to participate in the entire production process, for this reason we work with the outlined blocks or segments of the production cycle to determine the stakeholder's role over time. Another return-

'New, unknown or unfamiliar, directions'

ing issue in the co-creation processes is the monitoring of quality, although the process is of great importance to us, we also strive to deliver high quality outcomes. As one can imagine open ended processes and quality control can turn out to be a contradiction in terms. On the one hand we promote input from others while on the other hand we promote our 'own' high quality standards. Here we lean on the previously mentioned art projects that provide a pre-defined framework for interaction and we use the space between the cycles to jump between a user driven design, where the par-

ticipant can add, adjust and contribute to the process, and user centered design approaches, where the team members reflect and react on the input and adjust, and re-direct on the given material. In return this is brought back to the user driven cycle and is the next step for co-creation. This swapping game between the cycles challenges all involved creators, it uses the input but also allows for steps into new, unknown or unfamiliar, directions that might not have been at apparent at a first glance. In this way, the space and time between those cycles can be used as inspiration slots. It also

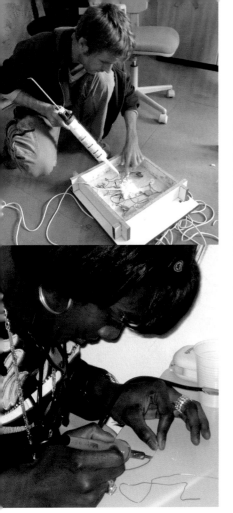

allows for new references and input that the others might not have been aware of, it uses user driven design and user centered design as tools *(Reiss, 2007)* that are appropriate for the development of high quality while still acknowledging the available expertise. It is not difficult to imagine these cycles could continue for ever after all; 'open ended' is never finished...

References

Star, S. L., Distributed artificial intelligence: vol. 2, Published by Morgan Kaufmann Publishers Inc. San Francisco, 1990

Reisss, E., www.lucamascaro.info/blog/user-experience/eric-reiss-user-centered-design-or-user-driven-design.html

Boal, A., Theatre of the Oppressed, London: Pluto Press, 1979

Muller, M. J., Participatory Design: The Third space in HCI, Published by Lawrence Erlbaum Associates Inc., 2002

Nigten, A., Art as Boundary Object? in (un)Common Ground, Creative Encounters Across Sectors and Disciplines, C. Brickwood, B. Ferran, D. Garcia, T. Putnam (eds.), BIS Publishers, 2007

Nigten, A., Processpatching, Defining new Methods in aRt&D, Lulu publishing, 2007-2009

Doorn van, M., Vries de, A.P., Co-creation in Ambient Narratives, in Ambient Intelligence for Everyday Life (AmI-Life'05), Lecture Notes in Computer Science 3964, 2006

Lewin, K., Action Research and Minority Problems, Journal of Social Issues 2, 1946

Buttler, D. and Reiss, V. (eds.), Art of Negotiation, Arts Council England in association with Cornerhouse, 2009

Recyle X: www.recycle-x.nl

Big South Lab: www.bigsouthlab.nl

Go for IT! city game: www.go-for-it-game.nl/

Thinking in the Middle of Things

Matthew Fuller

In her many-sided theorization of the history of programmability, Wendy Hui Kyung Chun proposes a way of working and reflecting on technology that she calls working in media res – in the middle of things.[1] Software cultures, according to Chun are best known through involvement, indeed nowadays, they can hardly be known from the outside. Something that characterizes the work of The Patching Zone is this thinking in the middle of things, but with a twist - that somehow, in everything they do there are many middles to be worked in, worked up and worked out. The Patching Zone thrives in the middles of technologies, knowledge practices, social situations, and in the invigorating tension of invention: what follows is an attempt to map some of these middles by means of a few vignettes.

1

A crucial problem that projects like The Patching Zone have to navigate is the way in which currently in the context of the ideological ascendancy of the 'creative industries', funding for media projects for 'excluded'

1   Wendy Hui Kyung Chun, Programmed Visions, The MIT Press, Cambridge, 2010

41

youth is often seen as something that means more 'basic' and perhaps less ostensibly glamorous initiatives are deprived of profile and funding.[2] This situation is amplified by the problem of stratification of education, which reduces peoples options, contributing to a situation where the gesture of learning to be a DJ or other avatar of the creative industries is seen as more exciting and likely of success than to be a car mechanic. Partly, this problematic tangles with the abrupt divisions of work in Dutch schooling, resulting in the idea that taking a gamble is better than risking a life of menial work.[3] This is a difficult policy to sustain en masse, but submission to meniality is unbearable. We are presented with another kind of middle, what Isabelle Stengers and Philippe Pignarre call an 'infernal alternative', a set of impossible choices[4]. Other ways out have to be found, and in parts, Rotterdam seems to have made itself a useful margin of experiment in ways to go beyond debasement or delusion as the

options for its young. Parallel initiatives such as Rotterdam Vakmanstadt with the renewed emphasis on meaningful, multi-layered skill, with a rich sense of the wider 'ecosophical' dimensions of life also provide a very useful sense of how this can be done.[5]

A significant way that The Patching Zone mitigates against being stuck in the regime of impossible choices is through collaboration with institutions that aim to think through the nature of common institutions and organizations in the digital era. The Culture Lokaal research effort, for instance, poses itself the problem of how to imagine the future of institutions such as libraries, youth services and schools. One of the crucial ways of reducing the infernal alternatives people face, is by multiplying the number of collective resources and avenues for expression.

Importantly too, The Patching Zone navigates this set of problems by integrating work teams. It sets challenging tasks for postgraduate students working with experts and with interested people from local communities. Thinking in the middle of things also implies working in relation to different paces, kinds and privileges in relation to different forms of knowledge. The question of how opportunities are made and are taken, couples with a need to understand questions of justice. This is something that is too much for any one

2   McRobbie A., Reflections on Precarious Work in the Cultural Sector, in, B. Lange et al, eds., Governance der Kreativwirtschaft, Transcript Verlag Bielfeld (2009)

3   Whilst there are many impressive aspects to education in The Netherlands, one of which is the significant degree of freedom for schools to generate their own educational practices, which, in the larger cities makes for the possibility of a real sense of education as being a collective intellectual project, by the time a child enters secondary education there is a strong set of stratifications taking place, with schools aimed at producing populations for various occupational kinds. This is in turn reinforced in higher education, with quite stark differences between the hogheschool (or polytechnic) and universities, re-enforcing and perpetuating social divisions.

4   Stengers, I. and Pignarre, Ph., Capitalist Sorcery, trans. Andrew Goffey, Continuum, London 2010

5   See, Rotterdam Vakmanstad, publiek onderzoek 2006-2008, Air Foundation, Rotterdam 2008, downloadable from www.henkoosterling.nl/rtd-vakmanstad.html and, Henk Oosterling, Woorden als Daden, Rotterdam Vakmanstad/Skillcity 2007-2009, Jap Sam Books, Heijningen, 2010

ing in the fresh winds rushing in off the North Sea. Connecting this endless supply of oxygen to the population of covertly dancing toes are the statuesque bodies of the Dutch, a people whom, at least since Mondriaan's Broadway Boogie Woogie, know, with uncannily intimate brilliance, how to dance to a grid. It is entirely fitting therefore that the dance moves set up by The Patching Zone's Go For It! project establish a means of linking this preternatural talent in a space that is at once both beach and grid, the pavements of Rotterdam Zuid. This project exemplifies thinking in the middle of things in a different way, it loads unexpected circuitry into the street, turning a patch of ground into something that elicits a new liveliness. The city becomes a site for interactive geometries to weave themselves and lets the beach trickle through the paving slabs at a slightly faster rate than usual.

project to bear, or to solve, but such problems can also be reworked in order that intuitions, structures, ways of speaking may amplify art or design's imperative to re-imagine the world in multiple directions.

3

One of the traditions in design that The Patching Zone resonates with is Participatory Design.[6] This current of work arose through the need to incorporate users of objects, buildings, places and systems into the processes of their commission and design at a fundamental level. In this way, the objects and processes that are introduced cleave more keenly to the requirements of the job that they do. But participation is not simply an efficient way of generating requirements and specifications, it is a way of thinking through design problems

2

The streets of Rotterdam, Gouda, Dordrecht are paved upon beaches carried back in from the coast and spread under cobbles and slabs. This something that gives Dutch towns and cities something of the ineffable air of a picnic. Such a mildly festive atmosphere maybe not entirely obvious, and is sometimes only palpable with a degree of effort, but there is a certain sense amongst the toes of the Netherlands that they may almost perceive themselves to nearing the verge of liking to slip off their shoes and have a wriggle on the beach. This happy atmosphere is occasionally also visible in the vivacity of the faces breath-

6   There is an extensive bibliography on the field, but see, Bjerknes, G., Ehn, P., & Kyng, M., (eds.), Computers and democracy: A Scandinavian challenge, Avebury Press, Aldershot, 1987

from inside the situation where they arise and in which they develop. It also requires a process of learning, and to a large degree embeds learning into the systems it yields.

Designers need to learn methods to draw out insights, observations and experiences from users. Users of systems need to learn to both step back from what they are used to in order to reflect upon it, but they also need to step into their habits, their usual work-arounds in order to reflexively think through their importance. As such, participation generates impulses towards a recognition of the sites it operates in, as sites of learning coupled with judgement and decisions. When things work well, such impulses proliferate out, setting up resonances with other scales and locations of life, in which the everyday, expertise, and processes of rethinking and imagination can be brought together.

This is when it works however, participation can also simply be a plug-in for defunct planning processes. It can find itself overloaded with problems generated by other domains, deep level problems that cannot readily be resolved by a phase of involvement or consultation.[7] At its best, The Patching Zone works in the thick of this set of problems, not by dodging them or black-boxing them, as beyond the possibility of timescale or budgetary reality but as something that runs through all work. Moreover, the way it does so is through recog-

nizing the partiality of all knowledge, that in processes of participatory design, everybody's knowledge is incomplete and in the process of atrophy or growth. The development of media systems is a particularly interesting context in which to pose these questions since they are both intimate and scalable, having implications that are both personal and operating at levels at which more generalistic speculations or conclusions can be made.

4

A further way in which The Patching Zone plunges into the middle of things therefore is to work with non-traditional clients, non-traditional or 'unfinished' experts, using non-traditional working methods in under-valued sites. It is, given this degree of compositional disequilibrium, somewhat unlikely that anything approaching an immediately easy life is produced. Working through the problem of generating a design or a process, finding the right way of going about things whilst keeping everyone on board can be frustrating. One way of responding is to react by people keeping their heads down, focusing on their technical limits, and functioning well within the skillbase. That makes sense, it makes you reliable and interpretable to others, builds your skills, but it may mean a project gets a bit stuck in cases where the professional domain needs to expand. How is it possible to stay focused and still be open-minded?

A slightly different way of doing things is exemplified by the Recycle-X project in Voorstraat in Dordrecht. Much of the work here is concerned with the inter-relation of informal city networks with low-key social movements

7   Lezaun, J., and Soneryd, L., Consulting Citizens: Technologies of Elicitation and the Mobility of Publics, with Linda Soneryd, Public Understanding of Science 16 (3): 279-297, 2007

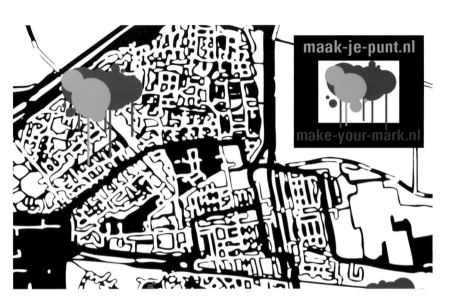

such as guerrilla gardening, and the renewal of older ones such as tinkering and old school locative media habits such as talking to your neighbors. This project inhabits many middles, of ecology, reverse gentrification, and the media practices it encourages.[8]

5

Peoples' lives are complicated, they are always in the middle of things, too busy to be interrupted, finding it difficult to really focus. It's necessary therefore that projects work also with things that aren't quite so distractable,

the expressive richness of everyday bits and bobs, a plant that can push its way up out of the ground without too many meetings to plan the process, a way of cobbling together designs from preexisting code and components. Thank god, in fact, that some work has gone on before.

The 'Processpatching' technique of The Patching Zone suggests a means of understanding the multi-layered nature of work in electronic art, a space composed of a matrix of influences, and recognizes that such work is made by being in the middle of development.[9] Skills, ideas and habits such as those of programmers, engineers, circuit benders, artists, researchers, and others align in different ways to yield particular projects. Long duration practices and

8 It is also open all the time – very much an affirmation of living in the thick of it. This may mean that a certain amount of energy for the project is drained by coping with life in the building, just keeping the place going while getting on with life may make things introverted at times. How can a project maintain a public openness whilst carrying out occasionally rather tricky technical development work?

9 See, Nigten, A., Processpatching, Defining new Methods in aRt&D, at www.processpatching.net

45

high level skills mix with buzzwords and the anaesthetic stupor of policy documents, momentary glimpses of opportunity, equipment, grant wrangling, schmoozing, mixing in turn with enthusiasm, street knowledge and the energies yielded by learning something new.

But thinking in the middle of things also means that the obdurance and activity of stuff: software, tables, buildings, books, addresses, plant pots, mesh networks, window cleaning cloths, the algorithmic richness of behaviour of wireless protocols,[10] add themselves to the mix. Thinking with things, what they can do, what they resist, and what happens when they break, also means to become aware of the subtle affordances and sympathetic liveliness of artifacts. This is something that has resonance both in terms of the everyday, but also in terms of the way in which computing and network technology is reworked, drawing it out of its boxes and into the thick of things. On the Recycle-X site, Kristina Andersen, blogs about a video by artist Koki Tanaka which minimally tweaks domestic objects into a new kind of insouciance simply by the minimal effort of a tender attention to detail.[11] She also proposes what she calls naïve electronics, an intuitive rather than logically driven approach to the generation of off-grid interactive artifacts that fuels itself on curiosity as much as the flow of electrons. Here the ability of circuits, sensors and many different kinds of current to teach us how to work with them in playful ways is what counts. Such attentiveness in the middle of things creates a context in which things are less mute, generating possibilities for many kinds of middle to find their edge.

------

10 For more on wireless protocols, see: Mackenzie, A., Intensive movement in wireless digital signal processing: from calculation to envelopment, Environment and Planning A, vol.41, page 1294-1308, 2009

11 rx.pr0be.info/node/76

Cultuur Lokaal

Cultuur Lokaal
January 2008 - July 2008

Commissioners / partners:	Waterwolf laboratories (Haagse Hogeschool lectoraat Society and ICT, Public Library Gouda, the Regional archive Central-Holland, Museum GoudA)
Target group:	Staff of the above mentioned, three cultural heritage institutes and the potential audience for these institutes.
Team:	Vincent Akkermans, Marcia Nancy Mauro-Flude, Mirella Misi, Corinna Pape, Vivian Wenli
Guest:	Piotr Adamczyk (US)
Mentors and staff:	Kristina Andersen, Marc Boon, Sandra Fauconnier, Lyndsey Housden, Anne Nigten, Sher Doruff, Dineke Keemink. Members of staff from the Gouda cultural institutes; Pim Bolsterlee, Social Work, Library Studies; Rosemarie de Heij, Library Mangement; Carolyt Koops, Library and Information Studies, Humanities; Jan Willem Klein, Dutch language and literature; Arjan van 't Riet, History and Civics; Hans Vogels, Art History; Ellie Wout, Library Programme; Julia Zwijnenburg, Museology and others; and their project manager Natasja Wehman, who has a background in Arts Policy.

Cultuur Lokaal is a collaboration between the Waterwolf project lead by Dick Rijken and The Patching Zone in The Netherlands. We are working with professionals in the three cultural institutes to investigate new opportunities for collaborations with (in)formal local networks. The Cultuur Lokaal project aims to inspire the cultural institutes to explore new ways to engage with the people in the street and local networks. We aim to address contemporary issues connected with the re-positioning of cultural institutes in the digital age. The investigation deals with the changing relation between professionals in the institutes and their audience as well as the role of the institutes in society. The work should encourage audience interaction and will be positioned where the museum and library rooms intersect with public and virtual space. The project will be developed according to a user-centered or participatory design approach. The project's thematic focus is media formats, local identity and audience participation. The physical location for the project workspace is in Gouda. A small group of six dedicated and prolific Master / PhD students from very different backgrounds work together for 6 months on the theme of local identity and the connection between the physical and virtual environment.

The anticipated project result is expected to be a well researched and documented, interactive experience in Gouda's (semi) public space. We will have the opportunity and the technological backup to work creatively with high-tech materials, digital media and information technology but use of technology is not a requirement in itself. The final project will be presented during a special public summer event in Gouda in July or August 2008, and afterwards there will be an opportunity to present papers or documentation of the research in a professional symposium in the early summer of 2008.

How the Cultuur Lokaal project was realised

The initial task for the Cultuur Lokaal team was to make it's own investigation of Gouda as a cultural and social place. We did this in a traditional fashion by researching the local statistics and official policies but more importantly the team explored the city by walking the streets and talking to shop owners, passers-by, beggars and street musicians. The picture that was drawn from this process became the inspiration for the way the team proceeded to work. We identified the market on the square as central to the city's idea of itself but also as a stage on which many of the underlying social and multi cultural issues play out. For this reason all of the experiments and interventions in Gouda were conducted either on the market square itself or in similar public spaces.

For each of these events a working group was established that consisted of The Patching Zone team and a selection of our collaboration partners, depending on the theme and location of the event as well as availability. The resulting teams then worked together to design, plan and realize each event.

The interventions of the Cultuur Lokaal project can be seen as a series where each action is in some way an elaboration and development from the actions that preceded it. In addition to this evolving narrative, each experience is setup and designed to explore a particular set of issues and concerns within the overall project, the interventions themselves are described by the participants in the following chapters.

Charming atavisms, new perspectives

Nancy Mauro-Flude 2010

In 2008 I was invited to work as a researcher for Cultuur Lokaal, The Patching Zone's pilot project in Gouda, The Netherlands. As a patcher the most remarkable feature of this project was the ability to contribute to the development of a method that aims to treat subjective phenomena and individual perceptions that occur below the official radar of Institutional Culture in a systemic fashion. To invigorate, as well as integrate new scenarios connected to local traditions that represent and respond to a specific community, we began to patch and to formulate conditions for what may be future models for effective collaborations between the general public, arts practitioners, media designers, and academic Institutes.

It's no secret that we are living through an era in which a change to the necessary structures on which art is supported and also distributed, discussed and consumed is taking place. These changes certainly have to do with technology and include new kinds of subjectivities that are co-emerging together with the creation of new platforms. It is a fact that peoples understanding of the definition of public space has been expanded through the inclusion of electronic

media spaces. For me the vital issue to explore in The Patching zone is that public domains cannot emerge spontaneously when the specific technologies are inaccessible and/or unfamiliar. Emergent technologies are often overwhelming – creating fear, uncertainty and desire in some people, and familiarity, curiosity and enchantment in others.

Acutely aware of these factors as a part of Cultuur Lokaal we produced five public events: CamERAMICS, Favoriete Boek Hoek, Vergeten Eten, Vergeet Me Niet! and Make Your Mark. In practice, through engaging and interacting with the locals of Gouda and the staff of the local Gouda Library, the Art Museum, Regional archives and Market Square, we were very much inclusive of local discourses that circulated around these communities and institutions. By paying special attention to etiquette - these events moved towards opening up the way that local craft knowledge is distributed in favor of collaboration and an acknowledgment of a broader community.

The projects I will describe brought people closer to technology on many different levels. All of these events dealt with the public domain as a mediated space consisting of both material and immaterial matter couched in the cultural phenomena existing in Gouda. I will elaborate upon these specific events below, but first I'd like to highlight these descriptions by drawing upon the significance of the term 'Patching Zone' and what it means to be a patcher.

I was attending the international conference 'Third Cycle: Artistic Research after Bologna' at Felix Meritis in October 2007 when I first heard of the project called 'Patching Zone'. I was

'Technology
is a well worn
tapestry'

enchanted by the term and envisioned a craft circle of people intensely stitching new, wonderful and enigmatic creations together. A patch can be both a piece of cloth or other material used to mend or strengthen a torn or weak point, and in computing it is a small piece of code inserted into a program to improve its functioning or to correct an error. Both a patch and a zone are part of something marked out from the rest of a larger whole, a particular characteristic is that they a small area or realm in themselves.

A patch is often worn by a member of a particular sub-culture within consumer society and traditionally is something that must be earned. By nature it makes a statement, confirms allegiances and promotes questions in a subtle but direct manner. Patchers choose not to buy new consumer goods; they fix old ones up, they reformulate and redefine, reuse, rehash, reconfigure, reposition the patch to make anew. Craft is always connected to technology, we can see this thread arching its way back through time, hence the word technology is derived from the Greek tekhne meaning art skill, craft, method, system.

Technology is a well worn tapestry of media innovation and technological design evolving in quantum leaps from the minds of few, it's bastard child, craft knowledge is cared for over time by the knowledge of many, which often causes ruptures between the two when really they are intimately tied. It is curious that patching tends to be mocked as a marginal and trivial activity.

The term patched up remains a powerfully derogatory expression, it is used as an insult, or to patch things back together gives connotations of a reunion or hope of reconciliation where there was formerly a tear.

The patcher is less likely to be seduced by gleaming promises of a technocratic utopian future. Instead an investigation into the way that things operate is conducted by the patcher, which goes right to the heart of human practice, that is, the tradition of being tool users and makers. In The Craftsman, Richard Sennett confirms this when he explains how 'Developments in high technology reflect an ancient model for craftsmanship but the reality on the ground is that people who aspire to be good craftsman are... misunderstood by social institutions (2008, page 145).' As patchers we worked to smooth this rift by creating a zone of experiential learning where local practices were both privileged and fore grounded. The trick to making it work was to bring outside researchers (from many corners of the globe) into the throw. This gave a renewed acknowledgment of local creativity in collaboration with specific local communities engendered via specific events and practices. And it became important to recognize differences within as well as beyond the participants of the patching zones borders and to acknowledge that a work of art or a cultural event can also begin a conversation between parties who might not see us as we see ourselves. Therefore an allowance for the different awarenesses and acknowledgements was afforded, putting a new spin upon specific practices and therefore developing new holistic models of creativity.

My training in ethnography has allowed me the freedom to work in a somewhat desultory fashion, likewise in 'Articulating the tacit dimension in art making', Michael Jarvis writes "if the current professional practice is to identify those aspects which are deemed to be 'good' or 'best' practice, then there is a danger that this will invite a host of imitators which will, in turn, deny opportunities for newer and more radical forms of practice" (2007, page 202). Broadening the definitions of creativity is a fraught subject that makes many people uncomfortable. It can be difficult to talk to them about the often invisible or subtle barriers of privilege that encircle the arts. Despite this we wanted to take emergent technologies and creative research out of the ivory tower into which it had floated and back into mainstream life, to free our project from the constraints of elite practice and to spread it throughout the lives and daily activities of the Gouda people. We intended to re invigorate what already existed but may have been forgotten within this culture, in this way local knowledge was rejuvenated and returned to the community. The selected researchers acted to appropriately reintroduce and reframe local customs and therefore begin a conversation about these cultural elements. I found myself searching in the nooks and crannies of Gouda, to gradually weave together stories of people and their practices, practices that had fallen beneath the official gaze of culture.

Patching as I mentioned implies craft, in particular a long claimed sensitivity to a direct sense of

connectivity to the physical world and that which immediately surrounds it, Gouda was formerly an invigorated realm, but its role as the first point of contact and centre for trade in Holland had long since ceased. The town in a sense had become a living anachronism. The resourceful use of old creative phenomena, revival of other ancient cultural industries that form a historical basis of what now constitutes craft and the integrity of the real world and its product, was acknowledged in the following ways in these specific projects:

1. Vergeet Me Niet!

This event was inspired by the Supernatural Drama film 'Afterlife' *(Wandafuru Raifu or Wonderful Life – Japan, 2001)*. Part scripted, part documentary, the film brings up questions of people's reality and memories and thereby forces the audience to contemplate the same questions themselves. Inspired by this, we decided to ask people for a memory related to a location in Gouda, which they did not want to forget. We simply asked, "What is the one memory related to a place in Gouda you would not want to forget?" We asked them to recount the memory in a few sentences before marking the location of the memory with a red circle mark on a large map of the city. We entered the exact wording of the memory into our 'memory machine' (computer), and then took a portrait of the person remembering that moment in front of the map. In order to turn the event into an exchange we provided people with a print of their portrait to take home and remember the event by. Every one who entered the tent was offered coffee or fresh mint tea. These basic staple drinks had with in them their own cultural protocols. Since the event was conducted on the market square this gesture received enthusiastic responses, all elements were free and therefore, to participate in the event was a good deal- something we were told was an important element for the people of Gouda.

During the event it became clear to us that none of our participants were used to being asked about their personal insight into the city in which they live. At first they all seemed to be genuinely grappling to answer the questions with actual memories. Their memories however brought not only new information about the city, but also showed the imbrications and layers that come into play when one talks about memory related to a city's tradition and history. An example is singing, which is a subject that keeps recurring in Gouda. There are 40 choirs and a young population of women that like to sing karaoke at 'Cafe New Orleans'. The other prominent city theme was cheese, but this obvious theme is only a small part of the life of Gouda and its villages, and it was striking to us that the myths we had been told about Gouda were not at all a part of the personal content revealed in the tent that day.

Vergeet ▼
Me
Niet

do 21-02-2008
grote rode tent
op het marktplein
gratis portret & thee

Een project van Cultuur Lokaal
http://cultuurlokaal.patchingzone.net

While many people had a hard time choosing which place they wanted to remember the most, this was not the case for everyone. A local woman came into the tent to ask about the project, and when we explained; she stood there for a while but left saying she would return later. When she did return to stand in front of the map, she slowly explained how so many things had changed in Gouda, small houses and buildings had been overtaken by global brands, companies and shops, and while she insisted that she did not want to forget anything, she could not bring herself to put her memories into our 'memory machine'.

The presence of the tent provided our visitors with a new type of space in which they could experience interiority while remaining in a public place. Our memory tent can be seen as what Michel Foucault defines as a heterotopia, in that it has the curious property of maintaining a physical relationship with other sites within the city but exists in such a way as to suspect, neutralize,

or invert this set of relations and what they happen to designate, mirror or reflect. Seeing our temporary tent as a site without clear geographical or cultural markers, affected a momentary relaxation of social identity that facilitated chance meetings and acted to liberate the conversation from the mundane stories of family or neighborhood.

Thus the journey into the tent provided the visitor with an 'outsider' experience of history that is in part nostalgic and in part a potent image of the dissatisfaction with the promises of an overbearing urban modernity. Weaving together the memory of a locality and the awareness of its present state enabled inhabitants to recall dreams and reaffirm desires for a simpler exchange within their community and signified a longing to revert to a somewhat ecological consciousness. The tent therefore was a manifold space patched on top of the public square that in the past has been a place of ancient myth, multifaceted humanistic exchange and cultural trade as much as it is today a site for tourism.

2. Vergeten Eten

The Vergeten Eten (Forgotten Food) event consisted of a stall on the market square in Gouda on one of the regular market days. The event was created and executed in collaboration with the Regional archive. The public was invited to taste ancient Dutch recipes and in turn to share their personal favorite meal. Specifically they were asked to write down; the name of the recipe, a list of ingredients, instructions on how it is made, and finally, the person who taught them to cook this. This final part especially stimulated much discussion. In the end we had not only a large and varied collection of recipes, but also a large repository of personal memories, which were produced through the collaborative dialogue that had been an intended by product of the production of the recipe cards.

In the back of the tent a group of workers from the Regional archive and the Public Library prepared two hot dishes: Gestoofde Spinazie and Aalbessen Sop. In doing so they literally performed an ancient process by following instructions from 16th century recipes that had been copied from originals in the Regional archive.

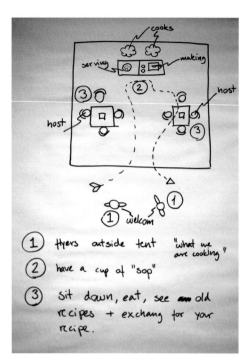

① flyers outside tent "what we are cooking"

② have a cup of "sop"

③ sit down, eat, see an old recipes + exchange for your recipe.

At two small tables in the tent, the visitor had the opportunity to taste Lavender Jam and explore a large collection of old Dutch recipes from the archive reproduced as recipe cards. Anyone was welcome to take a card home and in turn leave one with a recipe of his or her own. After the closing of the market all recipes, old and new, were added to an online website database to which others could contribute to or take from. The database grouped recipes in clusters based on ingredients, thus highlighting both their similarities and differences.

During the event the tent provided a space in which the performing chefs and recipe writers could enter into an intimate relationship. An examination of chosen recipes revealed the way the memory functions to frame specific cultural history through the experience of cuisine and facilitated an exploration of modes of representation encountered in the world of food and cooking. The relationship between the real ingredients of the meal and the fictional past is evoked through mending together a person's recollections and imaginations. Since experiences with food are universal theories can be readily constructed through examination of both an individuals relationship with it and that of a group as a whole.

What is curious about these old recipes when treated as cultural repositories, is that although development and change is primary, because time does not stop and everything in existence changes, especially organic matter, when it comes to recipes we solidify and reify something that in essence is always evolving, in statu nascendi. This process of organic development seems to take place outside of the chef's direct awareness and intention and is often governed by ex-

ternal factors. While exploring the process itself one encounters such issues as cultural custom, commerce and personal choice. Human experience is also deeply rooted in organic process. We perceive that what interests us and the periphery is dealt with automatically. So normally we do not pay any attention to the body's absorption of nutrients, our intestines deal with this quietly, but in the case of indigestion, we suddenly become aware of it. It's not like we were not processing the food before, we were simply unaware of the process.

An analysis of personal memories in relation cultural phenomenon allows us to approach behavior before it lends itself to utility and form before we separate an archetype from the physical realm. It was theorist Henry Bergson's conviction that immediate experience and intuition are significant factors in shaping our place within the world, and in fact lie at the heart of all acts of human creation, be it in the arts, in philosophy or in the sciences. Contrary to what people commonly think, this intuition signals effort, the effort to move against habitual, utilitarian thought.

3. Favoriete Boek Hoek

Favoriete Boek Hoek (Favorite Book Booth) took place at the re-opening of the Public Library Gouda in Bloemendaal. The booth allowed visitors to scan their favorite book's bar code and then pose for a picture holding the book in their hands. In practice the booth was installed in a corner of the library. As the person scanned the RFID barcode of the book, a light would go on and a picture was taken. This would go directly to a virtual picture album in the online flickr webpage. As the project's technician Mark Boon explains

"Technically the structure 'was hacked together' a single board microcontroller with Ethernet interface, a solid-state relay and a wall socket to form an Ethernet controlled power socket. It was used to switch on the lights of the photo booth when a photo was to be taken. The microcontroller board implements DHCP and NETBIOS, has a build-in web server and its I/O ports can be controlled by simple HTTP 'wget' requests. The optic-relay is connected to port F7, and a red LED is connected to port B6. By switching both the LED and the power socket on and off simultaneously, you have a visual indication if the socket is powered on or not." *(Boon, Marc. 2008, Preparation Conversation).*

Participants were also invited to leave a message in the form of a note on a scrap of paper inside

the book about why they particularly liked it, so that a larger dialogue between visitors of the library would be encouraged. In this way they would not only be able to gage one another's content preference and inclination, but also be stimulated to feel a stronger connection to their chosen book. The books in the library are re-read over and over again, and by enabling participants to leave small traces for the next reader, the aim of the event was to galvanize a sense of community between the local library users.

Through this process we ask can technology breathe new life into the urban environment and the public domain in a world where both the emerging virtual spaces and traditional urban space are increasingly being privatized and becoming more and more exclusive? We believe that now is the time to occupy space for public use, and develop it into a platform for the exchange of meaningful ideas and practices. Public space is by no means gone, we just have to look for it in different places.

4. CamERAMICS

The performance intervention CamERAMICS coincided with the annual 'Ceramics day' in collaboration with the Museum Gouda. On this day the main market square fills with tents in which artisans and collectors display their ceramics. On the terrace of the Gouda museum a large tent is erected where people bring their antique ceramics to be evaluated by specialists. The CamERAMICS event was a parody that played on the idea of the evaluation of ceramic objects with

performers playing fictional characters that embodied a mix of alien/ astronaut/ scientist/ anthropologist.
Four people were dressed in blue overalls, white gloves and huge goggles: two of them held small amplifier/speakers, one carried a mini video camera and one a laptop and a joystick as a human/computer interface devise. The troupe was linked by the wires of the objects/equipments, and walked together through the museum and around the market square. The performers approached the public and attempted to gage the emotional rather than the economical value of the treasured ceramic objects. A software patch was implemented on the hardware in such a way that the color patterns registered on the surface of the ceramics would trigger pre-made sound samples. The paint patterns and swirls on the ceramic objects were recorded with the mini camera, so that the sound of these objects would be transmitted through the small speakers held by the performers. Simultaneously both image and sound were displayed on a large screen in the gateway area of the museum.

Patterns into the next realm:
The process of creating CamERAMICS was based on ongoing group discussions about meaning, dramaturgy, aesthetic experience and the role of art and culture in society. By using concepts of software, interface and performance to rethink, redefine and re approach a specific cultural history and tradition, a situation emerged in which ceramics could be read and listened to rather than priced and measured. The interfaces were used on aesthetic and cultural forms specific to society in Gouda in order to bring about the possibility of new forms, new representations, and new symbols within that society.

"Conducting field research at the Museum's Ceramics Day trying to understand the complex relationships and hidden meanings that lie within the surface of their beloveds. As outsiders to Gouda and to the concept of ceramics - we are collecting and capturing this data to analyze and re-interpret." *(Wenli Li, Vivian, 2008)*.

The role traditional culture plays in contemporary society has changed in the last few decades through the development of communication technology, which brings us to ask what are the radically new representational techniques unique to our own time?

"Culture used to be a sector of the society, like economics, politics, ecology, health, and so on. The role of culture has changed in our contemporary society. The process of producing and giving meaning to human activities, that was the function of the cultural sector on a recent past, is now spread over a wide net of communication in witch the common citizen are able to share all sorts of information in a constant process of configuration and reconfiguration of meaning." *(Rijken, talk at Cultuur Lokaal, March, 2008)*.
How can we go about searching for these equivalents in society? Can there be forms specific to a

locale given that software and computer networks redefine the very concept of form and space? (Instead of being solid, stable, finite, discrete, and limited in space and time, new electronic forms are often variable, emergent, distributed, and not directly observable.)

"I like the futuristic element, since it allows lot of scope with the intervention into the event, these immaterial spaces created by imagination offers vital keys for others who need to comprehend such a change. What am I doing? Why am I there? What am I saying? These dramaturgical questions I am continually asking in my practice and related activities I am apart of. In regard to this ceramics project, I like the idea of the 'other time' character. It allows another type approach to the plates to make sense. This stimulates creative imagination of others, as only then do they get access to the ideas, learning and culture of others, past and present. If we are aliens or event people from another time researching (doesn't have to be so dramatic) then it makes more sense why we are engaging with these objects in unusual ways. I'm always bringing in extraordinary modes, drama and costume, of course; it's ok with a bit less. But it says something more than an everyday life type of approach. Field researchers from the future gives it more sense to why we are doing something surreal/abnormal with plates and of course it brings the time element into it, which the plates themselves are time repositories" *(Mauro-Flue, Nancy. 2008, preparation conversation)*

In the thought encountered in Debord's Derive, the Situationists', "transient passage through varied ambiences" depended on the delight of surprise *(Debord, 1996, page 22)* be it through preconceived improvisation, controlled happenstance or a strolling séance. Conversely the performers of the CamERAMICS event negotiated the annual urban plexus of Gouda on terms orchestrated only by their own hypnotic concerns. These wandering souls "dropped the usual motives for movement and let themselves be drawn by the attractions of the terrain and the encounters they find (found) there" *(Debord, 1996, page 23)*, so that dream and imagination could rein. The Derive can also be applied specifically to the process of scanning the old ceramics and jumping the groove of the patterns into the digital realm, reinterpreting them as audio to invigorate a quotidian ambience. Sound sculptor Brandon Labelle connects these peripatetic realignments of urban geographies with the making of sounds: "The derive becomes a model for making the pulsations and gyrations of perception, the very corporeal interpenetration of the self and the world... productive... within the space of sound-making is an ideological desire to immerse oneself in the re-imagining of a different set of relations... sound-making offers a way in which I may negotiate how I become a part of the world around me." *(Labelle, 1998)* Like Labelle's sound-making, CamERAMICS can be seen as "a kind of sonic-writing: a vocabulary (that) takes shape in the process of handling objects and producing sound." *(Labelle, 1998)*

Conclusion

The Patching Zone is not bound by what is officially accepted as art, it is everywhere and its definition is ripe for broadening and redefining. The projects methodology is a part of the inquiring approach to the material world and technology that includes scavenging, scrounging, tampering, adapting, fossicking, fixing. The museum, the archive, the library and the market place – all have their definitions of creative purpose that sometimes overlap and sometimes do not. However all of the activities I have described above share a common relationship to the local world and involve a cross section of inquiring minds to reappraise local artistic traditions. Whilst the imperatives may be different, both the community of The Patching Zone and the locals of Gouda took strong interest in the cultural practice and phenomena examined. A link was therefore formed between these groups: the layman and the professional. This thin but strong thread binds these communities through a process that goes to the fundamentals of both making things and innovation. It is to be found in a common interest in the open-ended investigation of the cultural world otherwise know as The Patching zone.

A participant of The Patching Zone wants to know why or how something works, not just because he or she is told that it is so and is the tradition. The Patching Zone may well provide answers to rebuilding a culture of resourcefulness recombining old and new technology into new forms driven not only by markets but also by human necessity.

References:

Debord, G., in, Theory of the dérive and other Situationist writings on the city, Andreotti & Costa (Eds.), Barcelona: Actar, 1996

Jarvis, M., Articulating the tacit Dimension in artmaking, Journal of Visual Arts Practice Volume 6 Number 3 Intellect Ltd, 2007

Labelle, B., Private Call-Public Speech: The Site of Language, the Language of Site in Writing aloud: the Sonics of Language (Eds.) Labelle, B. & Migone, C., Errant Bodies Press with Ground Fault Recordings, page 61-71, 2001

Sennett, R., The Craftsman, Yale University Press: New Haven: London, 2008

On Discrimination

Vivian Wenli Lin

Upon arrival in Gouda, the locals mentioned three things: that Gouda was a city without youth, without people of color, and on the perpetual brink of flooding. I decided to seek out the elusive immigrant community to hear of their experiences in Gouda and in The Netherlands.

"Holland was a really nice country, 15 years ago... it was really nice."

"You could communicate with everybody."
"But now they are a little bit scared of Muslims."
"The discrimination... since 10 years ago, since 11 September, the death of Theo van Gogh, the discrimination really..."

An aRt&D Method in Practice

Mirella Misi

"What strikes me is the fact that in our society,
art has become something, which is related only to
objects and not to individuals, or to life. That
art is something which is specialized or which
is done by experts who are artists. But couldn't
everyone's life become a work of art? Why should
the lamp or the house be an art object, but not
our life?" Michel Foucault. (1991).[1]

1   Rabinow, P., (ed.), On the genealogy of ethics: An overview of work in progress, In The Foucault Reader, Harmondsworth, Middlesex: Penguin, page 350, 1986

This paper focuses on the role of art and the methodological approach of working with artists to examine the impact of global economics and political processes on local cultural realities. Based on anthropological research and participatory art practices we suggest that the exploration of biographic/narratives in interactive art interventions creates a productive ground for an active public participation. For this purpose, we will draw on Michael Lingner's notion of Post-Autonomous Art (1992), Bouchenaud and Suri's concept of Experience Prototype, and Wenger, McDermott and Snyder (2002) concept of Communities of Practice to discuss the contribution of The Patching Zone method in its pilot project Cultuur Lokaal *(January to July 2008 – Gouda, Netherlands)*.

Introduction

An initiative of The Patching Zone and the Waterwolf laboratories (Haagse Hogeschool lectoraat Society and ICT – by Dick Rijken), the project Cultuur Lokaal was a practice research laboratory that examined the impact of global economic and political processes on this local cultural reality, by studying the cultural identity of the city of Gouda, in The Netherlands. Cultuur Lokaal was part of the BAM, a project of Gouda's government to integrate the three cultural institutions of the city, the Openbare Bibliotheek Gouda, the Regional archive Central-Holland and the Museum GoudA. Cultuur Lokaal adopted Dr Anne Nigten's Processpathing method of aRt&D, which is based on multi and interdisciplinary collaboration for basic research and experiments, having art as its method.

Research and Development in the Arts – aRt&D, is a term coined in 1998 by Nigten, then the director of the V2_Lab, to define practice-based artistic research in its relation to industrial R&D. As defined by Joke Brouwer, Arjen Mulder, and Anne Nigten on aRt&D: Research and Development in the New Art Practice, "is a critical consideration of the artistic, technical, and theoretical aspects of making electronic art in interdisciplinary collaborations, taking into account the cultural, social, and political-economic transformations that are the result of the widespread propagation of digital techniques".[2] It's related to R&D (Research and Development), in its purpose to create innovative forms of dealing with the professional development of workers and the improvement of products and procedures in the creative industry. What differs the aRt&D from R&D, in Nigten's words is that, "in a general sense, most R&D methods in industry and applied science focus on optimizing measurable processes or product improvement, and work with clearly outlined targets. However, in artistic research and development, the evaluation criteria are less clearly defined and there are no unique standards for measurement. In that sense, the aRt&D process resembles some aspects of basic scientific research.

While, different from basic research, aRt&D delivers working prototypes, processes or experiences" *(Nigten, 2006, page 07)*. In this Participatory Art Practice approach, The Patching Zone

method can be related to the concept of Post-Autonomous Art, as the German artist Michael Lingner defines it.

According to Lingner, the objective of a Post-autonomous art is not to create objects or to document the artistic creation process but to embody a political transformation and create an active space against the modes of production of Capitalism. Rather than a product, art is a space in which the participants experience a process of learning by exchanging ideas and concepts, crafts and techniques. In it's Participatory Art Practice, the Post-autonomous art opposes the way the social relations within this kind of axis are constructed, and seeks to potentially change those relations. It brings an approach to knowledge production as collaboratively made, not found, that in turn loosens the knowledge/power axis involved in knowledge production and expertness.

Art has become a system in society, and the contrast between the two does not exist any more in its old form. Today art's distance from society, its attempt to make itself independent as far as society is concerned, is completely illusory. Art can shape and develop its own particular nature only within society. Thus art-creation shifts into social communication. *(Lingner, 1992)*

In Cultuur Lokaal we proposed a mode of Participatory Art Practice on interactive installations, performance and video through Prototype Experiences. The objective was to promote public

participation and uplift social and cultural identity issues, bringing art closer to daily life. Our goal in the Cultuur Lokaal project, in line with the notion of Post-Automomous Art, was not to deliver a 'product' in the strict use of the term as an art object or interface design. We choose to work with Experience Prototypes for active engagement. The term 'Experience Prototype' emphasizes:

"The experiential aspect of whatever representations are needed to successfully (re)live or convey an experience with a product, space or system"; it refers to "any kind of representation, in any medium, that is designed to understand, explore or communicate what it might be like to engage with the product, space or system" at stake *(Buchenau and Suri, 2000)*[3].

In a larger consideration, the outcomes we were working on, in these experience prototypes, were the stimulation of Gouda's cultural dynamics and the cultural institutions' way of interacting with their public. For this reason, these experience prototypes had a focus on interactive participation of the public and an active participation of the institution's staff, both in the process of designing and in the promotion of the public events. An innovative way for the institutions to interact with their public was the final outcome we were to deliver. This brought us to consider that, in the case of the Cultuur Lokaal project, prototype experience was very close to a labora-

3   Buchenau, M. and Suri, J.F., Designing Interactive Systems, ACM: New York, 2000

tory for cultivation of a community of practice, involving the three cultural institutions. In a different way then, the design oriented approach to problem solving, the creation of communities of practice depends on the motivation of its participants, to stick together around interests and develop practices among common goals.

"Communities of practice are groups of people who share a concern, a set of problems, or a passion about a topic, and who deepen their knowledge and expertise in this area by interacting on a ongoing basis. *(Wenger, McDermott and Snyder, 2002)*[4]."

For cultivating a community of practice, its members must understand what the community is for; that is, the members must feel a sense of joint enterprise and accountability. Mutual engagement arises when members have time to build trust and relationships with one another through regular interactions. In addition, they develop a shared repertoire of stories, language, etc that embodies the distinctive knowledge of the community and allows members to negotiate meaning. In the negotiation of meaning, a community relies on the repertoire of practices intrinsic in their shared resources. In the Cultuur Locaal project, the memories of the citizens were the points of departure, to a travel in the shared resource repertoire of Gouda's identity.

One of the events we promoted in Gouda, Vergeteen Eten was an intervention placed in a tent on the market, on the market day in Gouda, the public was invited to taste an old recipe from the Regional archive, which was prepared and cooked fresh, in the tent. The members of the audience were also invited to write down one of their own favourite recipes in exchange for one from the archive. For that, the archive staff searched for regional traditional recipes, interpreted and translated them to contemporary Dutch, and made recipe cards to exchange with the public.

4   Wenger, E., McDermott, R. A., Snyder, W., Cultivating Communities of Practice: A Guide to Managing Knowledge, Published by Harvard Business Press, 2002

The act of cooking brought the personnel of the archive, out of the archive building and into the market place. The traditional idea of an archive could also be rethought, opening up space for innovation. The public participation brought the antique archive papers to life, lifting memories, revealing traces and stimulating the imagination. The role of the staff of the archive was shifted to perform the cooking. The audience acted also as performers, by writing down and explaining their own recipes. The role of intuition, spontaneity, improvisation and motivation were fundamental to experience this process of participatory interaction.

The habits around eating behaviours and culinary practices are related to the basic conditions of living of a given culture, such as climate, geography, believes, economic wealth, politics, and so on; which are determined by and in the mean time determinant of primary constitutive elements of cultural identity. Historically, the transmission of recipes allowed food to acquire its own language and grow into a complex cultural product, which can be investigated in many important levels of analysis of local cultures and in its relation to the global economy. The exchange of old and new recipes in this event could reveal a rich inventory of anthropological resource, contributing to the exchange of meaning within the community of practice by illuminating the

5   http://www.os.amsterdam.nl/pdf/2007_factsheets_1.pdf
    Lingner, M., Vom ende der kunstausstellung und ausstellungskunst Künstlerhaus Stuttgart (Hg.): 'META 2'. Stuttgart, 1992, Robinson, M., (Trans.). In: ask23.hfbk-hamburg.de/draft/archiv/ml_publikationen/kt92-13_en.html

peculiarities of its cultural identity and can be seen as a bridge between a social local network to a global one.

In research realized by the government of Amsterdam in 2007 – Creative Industry and ICT in Helsinki and Amsterdam: a comparison[5] – it is demonstrated that in both cities there is a clear relation between an urban (capital) atmosphere and the location of the creative industry and parts of the ICT. This confirms current theories of Richard Florida and others that the sector is being attracted by 'soft' location factors like tolerance, ethnic diversity, a lively (sub) cultural scene and attractive meeting places in the city. Although these social factors are the basic ingredients of web 2.0, and in spite of all the innovations that were made by the Internet and telecommunications (email, mobile phones, webcams, conference calls, wifi, weblogs, skype) and so on, the need for face-to-face contact remains and informs these new media applications.

The challenge of media democracy is to change the way information flows, the way we interact with the mass media and the way meaning is produced in our society. The production of meaning is central to the emergence and creation of identity at all levels, from the individual to the transnational. Meanings are encoded at the points of cultural production and negotiated and re-signified at the moment of consumption by the audience. Culture is a dynamic site of social context and interaction. The media does not shape social consciousness and behaviour as pretended by the media imperialism thesis, but conversely expands the flow of information in a multifaceted interactive live contest in which the production and circulation of meaning are intertwined.

We propose that embodiment is the central key to understand how our experience of living in the world is related with the qualities of our aesthetic experiences and those experiences shape what we call our identity. On a social level, we can derive from this hypothesis, that a local cultural identity is a sum of aesthetic experiences shared in the given community. The interrelation between local cultures can also be seen as a transcultural aesthetics experience that shapes a transcultural identity.

Ranti Tjan

Interview by Sam Nemeth

What was your first impression?

'The nice thing about my experience at The Patching Zone was that I didn't understand much of it at first: they came running in fully fledged, but it was totally unclear to me at least, what they were doing here. And actually that is exactly what you want as a museum of contemporary art: confusion and unclear situations because from there new things start. Also if we do not know how things are going to work out, and that also goes for the archive and the library, we are more curious about the outcomes and people become interested.

Ultimately this worked out well. The Patching Zone was an eye-opener, not only for the audience but also for the people that work here and myself. The Patching Zone proved to be an organization that experiments on a high level, often without knowing exactly where this will lead. Through their methodology they visualize the issues and the processes that lead to the end result.

How did you experience the method?

Yes, the method. It differs from other forms of brainstorming or lateral thinking or whatever

77

want to name it, those methods exist only in certain situations where you are sitting with your colleagues at a table and there's so much trust that you dare to think over your own borders. At The Patching Zone it is different: you are in the raw reality and there's trust, but there's also the hard reality that asks for a match and has to ultimately use your ideas, or partly your idea's.

There are many more stakeholders: locals, researchers, professionals or managers, to name a few, more than you will usually encounter at a round-table situation. You are working in a pressure-cooker, towards a new solution for a problem in a real situation.

For companies not very interested in theory, I think this is a golden opportunity to shift paradigms. To break out of ideas that have been holding a company back for a long time.

Thats also the innovative power in the Netherlands, in temporary combinations of science, art, design and business. Small informal constructions that together produce something big that could never have been done by a large conglomerate.

Relevance of Micro- Narratives

Corinna Pape

Keywords:

Micro-narratives

Lo-creative dialogue

Collaborative experience

Dialogical aesthetics

Performance art

This paper investigates the first three performances of the Cultuur Lokaal project in Gouda focusing on the various lo-creative dialogues that have been emerging between local people and three of Gouda's cultural institutions as well as within the mixed reality of urban and virtual space. From a narratological perspective, I argue that these dialogues are lo-creative dialogues since they are produced through a process of creating and exchanging micro-narratives on location. Thus, an analysis of the events will be done with the French narratologist Roland Barthes as the main theoretical foundation but with a displacement of the Barthesian focus from the fictional to the authentic text (personal stories from local people). Further, these personal stories were not only told as what Lyotard calls localised narratives or 'petits récits' (1984, page 60) functioning as a kind of folk sociology with a multiciplity of standpoints. They were also physically acted out as fragmented stories, with bodies as 'anecdotes' *(Brandstetter, 2000)*. This paper explores how these micro-narratives organized themselves both verbally and physically and hereby became part of the larger virtual dialogue in the lo-creative process between the cultural institutions and the people of Gouda.

1 Introduction

In 2008, the Cultuur Lokaal project aimed to inspire three of Gouda's cultural institutions (the Public Library Gouda, the Regional archive Central-Holland and the Museum GoudA) to investigate new ways to engage with people in the streets and (informal) local networks. In our digital age, cultural institutes are faced with changing relations between them and their audiences, and are forced to deal with the issue of making their collections more accessible. Over the last years, many cultural heritage institutions have undergone extensive digitalisation projects[1]. But as we found out through ethnographic research and personal interviews with locals, it seems that local people either refuse to go digital or that the massive amount of digitalized cultural content produces an illusion of access.

Therefore, the experiments we developed in collaboration with each cultural institution respectively had a particular interest in new communication media and methods: The dialogue we wanted to emerge was rather one that allowed for the audience to contribute to the collections than it was about how people access this information. Certainly, the latter was an effect of it. We created interventions as a way of 'remixing' the content that was provided by the institutions as well as 'lo-creating' different opinions and local stories from the audience. In all three experiments, we were eager to stimulate this kind of audience participation and deal with the issue of how to encourage people to tell their personal stories about Gouda, and how to make them aware that these stories were later on archived as well. This was critical since we wanted the audience to really start a sustainable dialogue with the institutions.

To get the audience engaged we used performance strategies that would encourage people to participate in our events. And to keep the experience from being one-sided we came up with the idea of exchange: People get a story from us and tell us their personal story about Gouda as a reward. By adding new technologies to the dialogical process, their own very personal local heritage, would become part of the cultural institution's collections and/or was later available online.

This opened up a whole new perspective on the dialogue that could evolve between cultural institutions and their audiences in the future – and provided a genuine 2.0 experience.

2 Research scope

This paper basically deals with the subject of lo-creative dialogue as a creative way of collaboratively producing local content. There were two research questions I was most concerned with during my work for The Patching Zone. The first one was: How does lo-creative dialogue evolve during the Cultuur Lokaal events? People who participated created their local content, micronarratives, which put them in touch with themselves, with others, changed their perspective towards their local surroundings. What becomes evident here is the rather aesthetic question of how to grasp the actual structure of these micro-narratives.

1 www.calimera.org/Lists/Country%20files/Netherlands_Country_Report.pdf

The second research question concerns the aftermath of both producing and archiving these stories by means of new technologies: How does lo-creative dialogue continue after the events?

3 The background

"We know that a text does not consist of a line of words [...] but is a space of many dimensions, in which are wedded and contested various kinds of writing, no one of which is original: the text is a tissue of citations, resulting from the thousand sources of culture."[2]
(Roland Barthes, The Death of the Author, 1967)

In "The Death of the Author", Barthes (1967) states that a writer can only imitate a gesture forever anterior, never original.[3] Any text, therefore, is deemed to be an alteration of older texts. These interrelations between texts, which are based on the concept of intertextuality[4], are essential when it comes to understanding the dialogic structure of any text, any narrative.
According to Barthes, the author's "only power is to combine the different kinds of writing, to oppose some by others, so as never to sustain himself by just one of them".[5] The reader, instead of passively reading a given text as a whole, is suggested to enter in the mode of the 'writerly' process: "The grouping of codes, as they enter into the work, into the movement of reading, constitute a braid [...]; each thread, each code, is a voice; these braided – or braiding – voices form the writing."[6] This 'writerly' process, as Barthes put it, is replete with multiple meaning: "the networks are many and interact, without any one of them being able to surpass the rest". This means: the text is open, "is a galaxy of signifiers, not a structure of signifieds; it has no beginning; it is reversible; we gain access to it by several entrances; none of which can be authoritatively declared to be the main one."[7] Herewith, Barthes dissociates himself from the notion of linear narration.
In fact, Barthes' goal is to interrupt texts and to illustrate that there is no necessity to begin a story at the beginning and proceed to the end. Therefore, he rather calls the texts he analyzes 'contiguous fragments'[8]. But while Barthes, being a structuralist, still holds the opinion, that every narrative employs organizational structures[9] which these 'fragments' relate to, poststruc-

2   Barthes, R.,The Death of the Author, 1967, page 52
3   Ibid.
4   In fact, the dialogic understanding of language is a major starting point for the poststructuralist concept of intertextuality, Julia Kristeva first introduced this term in her essay Word, Dialogue and Novel, 1969
5   Barthes, R., The Death of the Author, 1967, page 23
6   Barthes, R., S/Z. Translated by Richard Miller, New York, 1974, page 39
7   Ibid.
8   Ibid.
9   Barthes argues that any text is, in fact, marked by five codes, that each narrative weaves together in different ways: the hermeneutic code, the proairetic code, the semantic code, the symbolic code, and the cultural code. For further reading see: Barthes, R., S/Z. Translated by Richard Miller, New York, 1974

turalists like Deleuze and Guattari extended the idea of open texts towards their theory of a rhizomatic network structure that is intrinsically non-hierarchic[10]. This multiplicity also celebrates the many in contradiction to unitary, binary, and totalizing models of Western thought like grand narratives.

A grand narrative is an abstract idea that is supposed to be a comprehensive explanation of historical experience, a story about a story one could say, encompassing other 'little' stories within a totalizing scheme. Jean-Francois Lyotard criticizes and deconstructs the master narratives of modernity in 'The Postmodern Condition' (1979) stating that today master narratives have lost their power to convince us of the truth since they are literally stories that are told in order to legitimize a specific version of 'the truth'. According to Lyotard, master narratives should give way to micro-narratives, to 'petits récits' and more modest and 'localized' narratives. He suggests celebrating local and diverse forms of knowledge, esteeming dissension over consensus[11], and diversity over totality. He suggests that encounters across different cultural communities (and diverse forms of knowledge) should give rise to what he calls 'differends', incommensurabilities in which one party cannot make themselves understood. If this happens, Lyotard argues, conflict arises since every conversation is a contest and should be[12] and "to speak is to fight in the sense of playing"[13]. He claims that "what is important in a text is not what it means, but what it does and incites to do"[14] relating to Wittgenstein's phrase "The meaning of a word is its use"[15] – while Lyotard takes a step further referring to the importance of provoking conflict to embrace heterogenity.[16]

It is no coincidence that Lyotard borrows from Wittgenstein. In his work, Lyotard repeatedly invokes Wittgenstein's idea of the language game. In his most often quoted passage on language games, Lyotard writes: "The examination of language games [...] identifies and reinforces the separation of language from itself. There is no unity to language; there are islands of language, each of them ruled by a different regime, untranslatable into the others. This dispersion is good in itself, and ought to be respected. It is deadly when one phrase regime prevails over the others."[17]

---

10 Questioning the very existence of an origin (strictly speaking Barthes structure of codes), Deleuze and Guattari argue that all these fragments are interconnected just like a rhizome is as "any point of a rhizome can be connected to anything other, and must be." It is comprised of a multiplicity of lines and connections. See: Deleuze, G./Guattari, F., A Thousand Plateaus, page 13, 1987

11 Herewith, Lyotard dissociates himself from Habermas who always argued in favor of consensus. For further reading see: Crossley, N. / Roberts, J.M., After Habermas, New Perspectives on the Public Sphere, 2004.

12 Lyotard, J-F., The Postmodern Condition, page 175, 1984

13 Ibid. page 10.

14 Best, S. and Kellner, D., Postmodern Theory. Critical Interrogations, page 147, 1991

15 Wittgenstein, L., Tractatus Logico-Philosophicus, page 61, 1922

16 It is important to mention, however, that Wittgenstein's view poses a challenge to Lyotard's concept of conflict. Best and Kellner call his mode of analysis "Lyotard's one-sided celebration of differences, fragmentation and dissensus." Best, S. / Kellner, D., Postmodern Theory. Critical Interrogations, page 147, 1991

17 Lyotard, J-F., The Postmodern Explained, page 20, 1993

Wittgenstein's language games can also be borrowed here to understand the collaborative process that was at the bottom of creating narratives within Cultuur Lokaal. The practice always comes first, he once stated, meaning that the rules do not circumscribe the practice. Wittgenstein made clear that language games are intimately related to a context, or 'form of life'[18], which sustains them and gives them relevance. Considering Lyotard's bias against consensus, I argue that consensus can also mean answering a question or solving a problem collaboratively – for this is what we sincerely did within Cultuur Lokaal. While 'differends' *(Lyotard, 1984)* in fact existed, that did not mean, that we could not come up with a solution collaboratively – or, speaking with Lyotard, that all language games are incommensurable. We soon understood that during every creative process we had to speak out where we were coming from freeing ourselves from the patterns that confined us. We had to try to 'translate the untranslatable' *(Lyotard, 1993)* in order to invent a new form (of life, event, narrative) collaboratively. Rather than the content it was the context that was different or as Wittgenstein put it: "It is what human beings say that is true and false; and they agree in the language they use. That is not agreement in opinions but in form of life."[19]

The performances that took place within Cultuur Lokaal as well as the collaborative research process behind the scenes aspired to embrace and challenge diversity in such a way and discover new 'forms of life' encouraging participants to create language games within local-yet-foreign contexts. The stories we found and that found us were marked by encounters across different cultural communities in Gouda producing diverse forms of knowledge. These were indeed 'localised' narratives *(Lyotard)* created by the people. And as a result, their voices did form the writing *(Barthes)*.

4 The experiments

4.1 Vergeet Me Niet

The 'forget me not' (Vergeet Me Niet) tent[20] that was staged in cooperation with the Museum GoudA functioned as a memory tank aiming to preserve people's 'localized' narratives. Participants told us their favorite memory of Gouda and afterwards marked the location where it took place. There was no linear mode at all, participants could start at any point in the tent (in front of the map, in front of the camera, at the memory machine, etc.) to exchange their story with us. At the table, Vincent Akkermans typed in the words (Wittgenstein's "meaning of a word is its use" becomes ambiguous here) and they collaboratively produced a lo-creative narrative through dialogue. However, considering that participants were informed already outside the tent ('This is an art project') that they were acting within an artistic context, there is a chance

---

18 Wittgenstein, L., Tractatus Logico-Philosophicus. 1922.
19 According to Wittgenstein, form is the possibility of structure. Ibid.
20 During the first two Cultuur Lokaal events a red tent was placed on the market square of Gouda.

We asked people to tell us about a memory in relation to a place in Gouda they did not want to be forgotten and entered their story into our 'memory machine'.

Then Vivien Wenli Lin took a picture of the people remembering that moment, which they could take home. The pictures and stories were also available online later on. (cultuur-lokaal. patchingzone. net/ vergeetmeniet/ index.html)

Here the people would circle their remembered location on the photocopied map afterwards.

84

We exchanged more ancient Dutch recipes from our collection in the box with the audience (which they were able to take home) and asked them for a new one. They would write it on a blank recipe card, which was archived later on. (cultuurlokaal. patchingzone. net/ vergeteneten/)

Jac, Piepen-brock, Jan-Willem Klein and Joke Radstaat from the Regional archive prepared the two hot ancient Dutch recipes: Gestoofde Spinazie and Aalbessen sop. They literally performed the process of making an ancient recipe anew, of acting out the how-to's from our recipe cards to transform them into 'anecdotes' (Brandstetter): 'Anecdotes' which presented a repeatedly transforming image of the recipe.

they eventually did not tell Vincent Akkermans an authentic story. It is very likely that they left out certain parts or provided him and the 'memory machine' with only a fragmented story, a micro-narrative. By doing so and by telling us their fragments of memory, we used various language games bringing prominence to the fact that the speaking of language is part of an activity, or 'form of life'. We did as well use language games when calling our laptop a 'memory machine' and describing to the audience what it does since according to Wittgenstein language games are set up as 'objects of comparison'. Reporting an event or making up a story (and reading it) are - among a multiplicity – language games as well always containing both similarities and dissimilarities.[21]

But participants not only shared their memories verbally, they further acted them out physically in front of the camera as well as in front of the map. Much more than just memory mapping happens here. Gabriele Brandstetter describes how people reinvent themselves when confronted with an art context. They mentally draw themselves up as an 'artwork' (being both character and process). Thus, their bodies become 'anecdotes': presenting not representing an image that is always transforming, constantly deconstructing itself, impossible to grasp. [22] We decided that we did not want people to link their pictures with their circled location on the map afterwards to leave the actual memory as deconstructed as it happened to be inside the tent.[23] Participants just received their picture from Vivian Wenli Lin and could take their new layered memory home.

"A picture held us captive. And we could not get outside of it, for it lay in our language and language seemed to repeat it to us inexorably." *(Wittgenstein)* [24]

Later on, the database was built of a collection of all pictures made but people's micro-narratives appeared randomly and without linking them to the person that owned them in the tent. It could not be owned anymore, if at all. During lo-creative dialogue, it became part of the 'memory machine' and the map of Gouda. Therefore, micro-narratives appeared randomly in the database alluding to an idea of Barthes 'galaxy of signifiers'.

4.2 Vergeten Eten

During the 'forgotten food' (Vergeten Eten) event we invited people into our tent to taste an ancient Dutch recipe made by staff from the Regional archive and to share their favorite Dutch recipe. We asked them to write down the name of the recipe, who taught them to cook it, how it is made etc. Some participants actually talked us through the whole cooking process, others

---

21 For further reading see: Wittgenstein, L., Tractatus Logico-Philosophicus, page 130, 1922

22 For further reading see: Brandstetter, G., Der Körper als Anekdote, Beobachtungen zum Bewegungstheater der 90er Jahre, page 403-422, 2000

23 According to Ranti Tjan, Director of Museum GoudA, it is crucial today, to find new ways of exhibiting, i.e. by leaving character tables next to a painting or sculpture blank to avoid predesignated meaning.

24 Wittgenstein, L., Tractatus Logico-Philosophicus, page 115, 1922

We asked people to look for their favorite book
in the library and to bring it to our booth. Then
they would scan the code of their book.

only told us whom they learnt it from and wrote the ingredients on a recipe card. Not only did we have a collection of recipes in the end, but a collection of micro-narratives produced through collaborative dialogue.

Greeting people outside the tent, speculating with them about the food, describing the appearance of a special food, thanking them for participating are all language games. Again, for people who understood the artistic context of our event and who entered the tent (sharing a specific 'form of life' with us) it was easy to play along different language games and to create micro-narratives (both verbally and physically while in fact cooking and eating with us). Others were skeptical (i.e. about the free food), evoking 'conflict' *(Lyotard)* which was rather useful for the purpose of reflecting upon and revising existing conventions and forms of practice. In this perspective, one can frame Vergeten Eten as a process that sets the stage and the conditions for a series of micro-narratives that are triggered by engaging with localized content.

By photocopying the recipes (in ancient Dutch writing), which are stored in the Regional archive and by not showing the authentic cooking books they were in, we intended to negate their origin and avoided putting them in the scope of a meta-narrative.

Later on, all recipes were available online in a database that most likely presented the idea of a rhizomatic structure *(Deleuze and Guattari)* in which any ingredient was interconnected to the other and every recipe was interconnected as well. People were also able to add more recipes to this database.

We encouraged them to take a picture in front of our booth with their chosen book. These were available online later on. (www.flickr.com/photos/smoelenboek)

4.3 Favoriete Boek Hoek

The third event 'favorite book booth' (Favoriete Boek Hoek) took place at the re-opening of the Public Library Gouda in Bloemendaal. We let visitors scan their favorite book's barcode and asked them to pose for a picture holding the book in their hands. Our idea was that participants could also leave a message inside the book about why they liked this particular one so that dialogue between visitors of the library would be encouraged. More micro-narratives would thus be added to the book and both the library and the local people would feel a stronger connection to each other since they would know about people's favorites.

To make participants feel a stronger connection to their chosen book, we wanted them to scan the abstract code and make a picture of themselves holding it. This also adds to Brandstetter's notion of the "body as an anecdote".

Looking at all the pictures people took together with their books, I remember Barthes theory that a text's unity lies not in its origin but in its destination. The books in the library are re-read over and over again, and by enabling participants to leave small micro-narratives for the next reader, we wanted the event to create dialogue and leave traces of community.

Pictures online were captioned with the book's code. Watching them on flickr later on contributed to the feeling of having physically left traces of community.

Conclusions

Postmodernism questions the major cultural and aesthetic theories to the benefit of a constellation of 'small stories', micro-narratives, which are rich in nuances and evoke a world that is literally closer to our 'small realities' yet being also more complex and more subtle, more informal.

Lo-creative dialogue produced by micro-narratives that are created, shared and acted out at the location where they indeed took place will thus contribute to a richer dialogue between local people and the cultural institutions. When confronted with an artistic context or a specific 'form of life' (Lyotard) by means of a performance which people are able to join, they are offered a stage to playfully engage with language games in order to create a diversity of micro-narratives. People would tell their own 'localized' narrative, share personal story fragments about Gouda, share opinions and give recommendations. Local people were also encouraged to perform and physically act out their micro-narratives anew using technology (Vergeet Me Niet) reflecting on the process of creating personal cultural heritage. When these micro-narratives were available online for the public later, people were able to again add content (Vergeten Eten) and get in touch with other participants (Favoriete Boek Hoek).

Attention was paid to people's lives in Gouda, emphasis on their daily reality, interest in a universal form of introspection, the desire to tap into and map and share micro-narratives on the basis of small realities to enable poetic imagination. All this was at the heart of the work done within Cultuur Lokaal.

References:
Barthes, R., The Death of the Author, 1967
Barthes, R., S/Z. Translated by Richard Miller, (New York), 1974
Best, S. / Kellner, D., Postmodern Theory, Critical Interrogations, 1991
Brandstetter, G., Der Körper als Anekdote, Beobachtungen zum Bewegungstheater der 90er Jahre, 2000
Crossley, N./Roberts, J., After Habermas, New Perspectives on the Public Sphere, 2004
Deleuze, G./Guattari, F., A Thousand Plateaus, 1987
Kristeva, J., Word, Dialogue and Novel, 1969
Lyotard, J., The Postmodern Condition, 1984
Lyotard, J., The Postmodern Explained, 1993
Wittgenstein, L., Tractatus Logico-Philosophicus, 1922

Partners:

GO FOR IT!

Go for it!

| Keywords: | Game design, art interventions, urban culture, mobile technology, social aspects of public space. |

Go for IT!

January 2009 - end 2009

Location:	in public space, borough of Feijenoord, Rotterdam (NL)
Commissioners / funders:	Rotterdam South Pact, CCC programme by the Dutch Ministry of Economic affairs and the Dutch Ministry of Education, Culture and Science
Partners:	SWF youth workers, Nieuwe Kans, SBAW, borough of Feijenoord, Kosmopolis Rotterdam
Target group:	Young people, ages 13–20
Genre:	City dance game
Team (full-time and part-time):	Christopher Baronavski, Pinar Temiz, Thomas Duc, Andreas Zingerle, Selena Savic, Andreas Muk Haider, Konstantin Leonenko , Asmidin Visser, Moneba Malik
Work experience team-members:	Marvin Gomes, Dennis Dressman, Geoffrey Frimpong
Guests:	Huan-ling Chen (TW), Elizabeth Cairn (CA), Varvara Guljajeva (AT)
Mentors and staff:	Lyndsey Housden, Kristina Anderson, Lynda Hardman, Sam Nemeth, René Wassenburg, Simon de Bakker, Dineke Keemink, Anne Nigten
Technical assistance:	Xavi Amoros, Stijn van Beek, Tim Walther, Jan Trüzschler von Falkenstein

Go for IT! is a creative collaboration project that will be developed for and with the youth, students and researchers in Rotterdam South. The project is built around a series of creative technology workshops and public events that deal with contemporary technology such as 'wearables', electronics, e-fashion, mobile communication and other expressive means. The outcome of the workshops and events results in an interactive Urban Game that will be performed and played in a public space in South Rotterdam's city district Feijenoord. The project will be realised, under the supervision of professionals, as a collaborative effort by local young people and a team of outstanding students from different backgrounds. The objective of Go for IT! is multifaceted, we aim to work on several social issues such as exchange and collaboration amongst young people; national and international students; professionals from the creative industries; and the promotion of creative urban youth culture. We plan to make connections with innovative urban game concepts and technology relating to public space. This brings forward the most pressing issues to be worked on within Go for IT! How can game concepts, art, and cultural events be of value for the enrichment of public space? Which creative technology applications could encourage co-creation and collaboration in urban public space?

And how it was developed

The Patching Zone produced the Go-for-IT! city game project in 2009/2010. During the process several playful elements were devised and produced, which resulted in a city game that is played on several fields consisting of ordinary street tiles with LED's and sensors. Several team members were designers and electronic engineers as well as artists from all parts of the world, from the United States to the Ukraine. It took a while to get on common ground, because of all cultural and professional differences and the playfulness of the project played a role in this.

The project started from an action research approach, using a communal research phase to decide what the vantage points for a city game would be. Questions like; what platform does the target group already use and what games do they play, were answered by people from the neighbourhood during research at the local sports hall and community centre. The outcomes of these street interviews were too thin and it was hard to gather useful information. From there on an experiential action research form was preferred, the team organized workshops where not only the target group participated, also the team, to play a range of games. This not only brought a light atmosphere, it was also fun and broke the ice.

The workshops were all built around doing, playing and making. Although each workshop was different in it's set up and topic, they all shared a two-fold objective; firstly the workshops worked as an introduction of our team and our work to the youth, they were encouraged to play, test and start creative experiments with technology as a communal act etc. And secondly our team was able to get to know the target group, gather information about the young people's preferences, media usage patterns, interests and taste. The workshops stretched from low tech to high-end; from music making with potatoes, constructing wearables with paperclips and LED's, to electronic music making, testing of dance and movement games, and playing a QR game in the streets of Rotterdam South.

Based on these experiences, the team devised simple games themselves and on several occasions presented mock-ups to the target group as an initial user test. Among the outcomes of these events, with fancy names such as the big game test, included information about the youths' game preferences. The game elements that proved interesting to the target group were

- Interaction by moving (dancing)
- Eye-hand (eye-body) control
- Stamina: rudimentary games where ones physical condition as well as ones precision in interacting determines the success.

The team set out to build several prototypes that incorporated these elements, based on literature and research concerning safety and availability of technologies. A number of iterations lead to a final design that stimulates both communication and interaction, not only with the game interface but also between the players.

Go-for-IT! is designed as a dance game that focuses on several skills, (there are several games for the platform) on 4 different locations in Rotterdam South. The emphasis is on short, competitive gaming but there are a number of very young kids, from 7 till 11 years old, that use the setup for open-ended playing. The team is not surprised by this because although aimed at an older target group, Go-for-IT! is designed to facilitate a range of gaming possibilities, including playing with the interface, appropriating your own meaning to the light patterns and so on.

Tic-TAG-Toe

Christopher Baronavski

Early in 2009, the Go For It! team developed an intuitive, yet highly addictive multi-player permutation of the classic tic-tac-toe paradigm, which evolved from research enquiries exploring movement and cooperative strategizing within urban public gaming. Departing from the traditional naughts and crosses emblematic of the 2-dimensional archetype, large alternately-coloured cubic game pieces are arranged on a physical 3 x 3 grid by two teams. Fast-paced games of Tic-TAG-Toe enhance players' reflexes, endurance, strategic thinking, and communication skills. Fun to watch, easy to learn, yet immensely challenging, Tic-TAG-Toe became an instant hit with both kids and adults.

Gameplay

The objective of the game is identical to that of tic-tac-toe; be the first to align 3 of your pieces on the grid in a row, column, or diagonally. 5 participants are required, including 4 players split into 2 teams, as well as 1 arbiter who presides over the match. A 3 x 3 grid with a total surface area of approximately 9 square meters is drawn with chalk or tape. Both teams and their cubes are initially stationed in a home base situated outside one edge of the gridded court. Only one player from each team may enter the grid at any given time, although both teams may make their moves simultaneously. Each team consists of a Maker and a Breaker. Makers must place their team's game piece on a single cell of the grid as quickly as possible before returning to home base to pick up another piece. The Maker may place her team's piece on a cell adjacent to the opponent's piece to block the opponents' attempt to build a winning configuration. Alternatively, the Maker can tag her teammate, the Breaker who may then enter the grid and remove one of their opponent's pieces. When the Breaker tags her teammate, the Maker is once again activated. The first team to arrange 3 of their pieces in a row, column, or diagonally wins the match. An arbiter overseeing the game ensures that both teams adhere to the rules and determines the winning team.

Because game pieces can be reconfigured many times, Tic-TAG-Toe is much more open-ended than it's progenitor, in which the winner will usually manifest after very few moves. In traditional tac-tac-toe, the first move advantage is difficult for the opponent to overcome, and if both players are experienced, a tie will almost surely result, excepting for carelessness or negligence. However, a number of different strategies will emerge during the course of a game of Tic-TAG-Toe. A brute force strategy, which depends upon an agile Maker placing pieces on squares closest to the home base, can easily be countered by the opposing team's Breaker. A more defensive strategy might entail placing pieces further from the home base to make these pieces more time-consuming for the Breaker to retrieve. Even when one player tags out, she remains engaged in the ongoing play, monitoring the moves of the opponents and advising her teammate accordingly. Cultivating adaptive anticipatory strategies, keen physical and mental reflexes, and ongoing communication and cooperation with team members are integral to success.

Results

During an initial rollout at a youth center in the South of Rotterdam, Tic-TAG-Toe was received with immediate and uniform acclaim by youths and adults, attracting a large enthusiastic crowd. Even after playing several rounds, players would queue to compete again. In fact, after the Go For It! team disassembled the game, hours later we returned to discover that players had reconstructed the arena and formed a sort of quasi- tournament, this was certainly an encouraging development.

The strength of the game lies in its fusion of team-based physical activity with prototypical, readily comprehensible gameplay. Most school age children, regardless of their individual cultural backgrounds are proficient in tic-tac-toe, and even the various strategies that may be utilized. However, as Australian mathematics educator Philip Clarkson notes, even the practiced tic-tac-toe player may be wholly unaware that she is engaging these strategies.[1] A cooperative gameplay model encourages players to flexibly deploy multiple strategies, as well as to articulate

these to her teammate. Additionally, the time-sensitive component of the game fosters rapid exploitation of these critical thinking and decision making skills.

The facile parameters of the game are easily modified to accommodate varying age ranges and degrees of ability, by altering the dimensions of the grid, the physical properties of the game pieces, or even the number of players per team. Smaller children may benefit from smaller or differently shaped game pieces, as we found the standard size (roughly 50 cm in diameter) somewhat cumbersome for these players to manipulate. Additionally, older players seeking a more formidable challenge could employ weighted game pieces. Another variation on basic gameplay might allow the stacking of game pieces on single cells of the grid, adding an additional set of potential winning configurations and facilitating truly 3-dimensional gameplay. Most of all, players are encouraged to think of themselves as 'co-creators', given the freedom to experiment with the game's structural characteristics

This corresponds to the unmistakable conclusion of the research conducted by Go For It!: It behooves public gaming initiatives to investigate new gameplay scenarios, which interconnect with and evolve from the domain of gamers personal knowledge and experience of play. Summoning a simple yet universally understood gameplay and turning it to accommodate a specific milieu can yield fantastic results. Undeniably, there is a fundamental appeal for archaic games, which still remain, enjoyable and challenging despite the succession of millennia.

1 Clarkson, P. C., Exploring the possibilities of using tic-tac-toe to think and communicate about mathematics, Australian Mathematics Teacher 64 (2), 2008

concealed color lay out

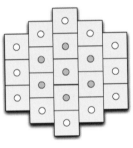

selected color

concealed color lay out

life indicators: turn red if life lost!

revealed color lay out

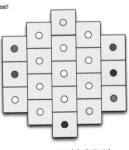

revealed color lay out

Game Design Sketches

Andreas Zingerle and Pinar Temiz

Focus

This game is about memory skills, thinking & reacting.

- -

MODES: It can be played by 1 player or 2 players (PvP)
OTHER: The game experience is supported by music that is transmitted over the mobile phone. Duration of one 'round' (not level) is approximately 2:00 minutes, and is indicated by the music that is playing.

BASIC RULES:

1) Players should stand on the green lights.
2) Players have to memorize the arrangement of the coloured lights.
3) The colour layout is concealed and players have to find all the lights in the selected colour.
4) If they miss they lose a life. If they find all the lights in the selected colour they gain 1 focus point.

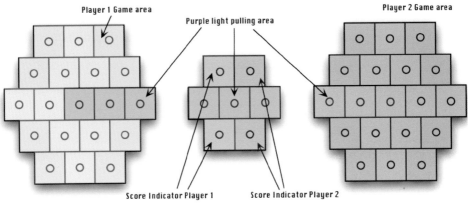

Player 1 Game area

Purple light pulling area

Player 2 Game area

Score Indicator Player 1

Score Indicator Player 2

STAMINA
BURGEMEESTER HOFFMANPLEIN

Stamina

This game aims to challenge the player(s) endurance, with high intensity action; how long can you keep going.

- -

MODES: It can be played by 1 player (against system/environment : PvE) or 2 players (against each other: PvP)

OTHER: The game experience is supported by music that is transmitted over the player's mobile phone. Duration of one 'round' (not level) is approximately 2:30 minutes, and is indicated by the music that is playing.

BASIC RULES:

1) Player has to step on the green lights.

2) By stepping on the green lights, the purple light will be pulled in their game area. The player with the most collected purple lights wins the round. As you can see in the layout, each player has their own game area (game pads indicated in green and blue). The horizontal purple line (9 tiles) indicates the area where the purple light is pulled. The 4 tiles in the middle field (Score Player Indicator) shows when each player scores a point.

REFLEX
MALLEGRT

Reflex

This game is aiming to challenge the player(s) on their reflex skills.

- -

MODES: It can be played by 1 player (against system/environment: PvE), 2 players (against each other: PvP)

OTHER: The game experience is supported by music that is transmitted over the mobile phone. Duration of one 'round' (not level) is approximately 2:00 minutes, and is indicated by the music that is playing.

BASIC RULES:

1) Player has to dodge the red lights.
2) Player has to catch the orange lights (by stepping on them). The white lights in the corner indicate the life situation of the player.

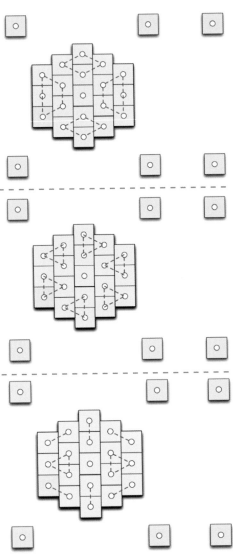

Groove

This game challenges the player(s) timing and rhythm skills. The goal of the game is to move yourself in sync to the lights and music.

MODES: It can be played by 1 player (against system/environment: PvE), 2 players (against each other: PvP)

BASIC RULES:

The goal of the game is to move yourself in sync to the lights and music. Green areas will light up and the player has to step on them. Pink lights will randomly light up and when stepped on players can collect bonus points.

If the player misses a beat by not stepping in time to the green light rhythm, they will loose 1 life point. When all the lives are lost, the game ends.

Go for IT!
System
overview

Simon de Bakker

Figure 1
Go for IT! system components

The Go for IT! system is a complex system built utilizing a modular topology. Figure 1 shows the different components the system comprises of. This chapter describes the functionality of each component and how it relates to the rest of the system. The main form of communication between the different modules is by means of TCP/IP. For ease of implementation and uniformity Go for IT! modules all communicate using the same protocol and datagram format (Figure 2).

Asterisk PBX

"Asterisk is a software implementation of a telephone private branch exchange (PBX) originally created in 1999 by Mark Spencer of Digium. Like any PBX, it allows attached telephones to make calls to one another, and to connect to other telephone services including the public

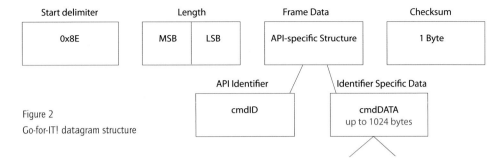

Figure 2
Go-for-IT! datagram structure

switched telephone network (PSTN) and Voice over Internet Protocol (VoIP) services."
The Go for IT! Asterisk PBX's main functionality is that of an Interactive Voice Response (IVR) system. It is the main means of communication between the user and the system. The IVR is implemented as a set of Asterisk Gateway Interface (AGI) scripts located in the Asterisk AGI directory.[1]

Table 1
Go for IT! AGI implementations

Script name	Triggered by	Actions	Script language
pz-incoming.agi	incoming call at 0800- extension	connect to brainproxy present IVR system terminate call	C language
pz-incoming-single.agi	incoming call at 0800- extension	connect to brainproxy present IVR system single player only (no mode selection menu)	C language
pz-outgoing.agi	outbound call via goforit-outbound context	connect to brainproxy present IVR system stream music (music on hold) terminate call	C language
pz-failed.agi	failure during outbound call via **goforit-outbound** context	connect to brainproxy send HANGUP with reason	C language
smsscore.agi	successful ending of pz-outgoing.agi	Send SMS through the SMS gateway.	Bash
smsfailed.agi	failure during outbound call via **goforit-outbound** context	Send SMS through the SMS gateway.	Bash

---

1   Exact location of this directory depends on the Asterisk installation and can be found in the configuration files.

BrainProxy

The AGI scripts used in the Asterisk PBX do not contain much intelligence and logic. This is accounted for by the Brain, which will be described in the next section. The AGI scripts need some means to communicate with the Brain application. All communication passes through the BrainProxy.

Because the AGI scripts don't have a notion of each other the BrainProxy was introduced. The BrainProxy is meant to streamline all communication from all AGIs to a single Brain connection. Moreover the BrainProxy assures that messages from the Brain are routed to the correct AGI. This is especially important during multi-player mode games. Secondly the BrainProxy sets up the outbound telephone connection when requested by the Brain (after receiving a valid location verifier).

Besides these, the BrainProxy just acts as a funnel for the AGI to Brain and as a router for the Brain to AGI communication, leaving the datagrams intact.

The Brain (game hub)

This is the module responsible for all user accounting, communications and statistics. In short the Brain is the central organ where all other modules operate through.

The Brain is responsible for a number of different tasks:
* Location management
* User management
* Game communication
* SMS Sending[2]

Location management

Only a finite number of players can play on a location simultaneously. In the current implementation that is 2 single players or 1 pair of players in multi-player mode. At the moment of calling the system does not know at which location the caller is situated[3]. The caller is presented with a voice menu allowing her to choose her location. The location is checked against the database to see if a game is already going, if is operational etc., after which the caller can continue or is advised to try again later.

Location requests are kept in the database on calling and removed on call termination with the exception of call termination on the waiting for steps event issued by the game location. This is

---

2   SMS sending on the Brain side is not yet implemented although the stubs are there. SMSs are sent via the Asterisk AGI interface at the moment of writing.

3   This could be simplified by the use of a different 0800-number for each location and a point of research for the second phase.

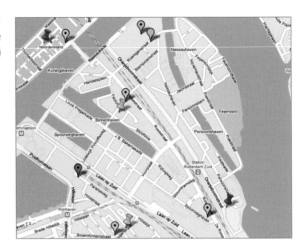

Figure 3
ZigBee locations (pins are game
locations)

the event type where the Brain reserves the location and requests the caller to perform an action on the playground to verify she actually is physically present. If this action is not performed within a certain time frame the location request is dropped and the location freed for other callers.

User management
Upon calling the CID is linked with a unique id, which is used as identifier within all other communication. This coupling is persistent in between calls and stored within the Brain database. During a complete game cycle the id is linked with a location. This link is lost on call termination (game end).

Game communication
The Brain is the only module that communicates with the game locations through the ZigBee gateway (described in the next section). The only exception to this is the BrainProxy, which sends exactly one message (ZIGBEE_START) to the game locations to start the game on location. Because there is no syncing between the game on location and the music that is played through the Asterisk PBX the music and game need to be started as simultaneous as possible (this is especially important for the Groove game as with this game scoring is dependent on being 'in beat'). With the START_GAME message, originating from the Brain directed to the BrainProxy, an average network delay for the location is passed as an argument. The BrainProxy uses this delay to time the start of the music and the start of the game on location.

Figure 4
Remote network health monitoring.

GATEWAY

name	PAN	serial
GAME_COORDINATOR		0x00000000013a200

GAME LOCATIONS

name	active	last seen	network identifier	mac address (64bit)	network address (16bit)	old network address (16bit)	response time (s)	supply voltage (v)
Hoffmanplein	false				ffe		0.000	0.000
Pincoffsweg	true	Sun Jul 25 11:58:07 +0200 2010	HOFFMANPLEIN		1f5c		0.107	0.000
Mallegat	false				ffe		0.000	0.000
Paulkrugerstr.	false				ffe		0.000	0.000

ROUTERS

name	active	last seen	network identifier	mac address (64bit)	network address (16bit)	old network address (16bit)	response time (s)	supply voltage (v)
Unilever	true	Sun Jul 25 11:58:27 +0200 2010	3071JL_UNILEVER		080d		0.086	0.000
Albeda college	true	Sun Jul 25 11:58:27 +0200 2010	3071AL_ALBEDA		2b23		0.091	0.000
1989	false				ffe		0.000	0.000
Noordereiland	true	Sun Jul 25 11:58:37 +0200 2010	NOORDEREILAND		1a9d		0.094	0.000
Hilledijk	true	Sun Jul 25 11:58:38 +0200 2010	3072HA_HILLEDIJK		4029		0.097	0.000
Paperclip	true	Sun Jul 25 11:58:38 +0200 2010	BUILDING_PAPERCLIP		1a55		0.101	0.000

ZigBee network

For communication with the remote game locations a ZigBee network is laid out over the South of Rotterdam (see Figure 3). Go for IT! is based on a mesh topology with one ZigBee coordinator several routers and 4 end-points representing the game locations.

The ZigBee coordinator simultaneously acts as an Internet gateway connecting the ZigBee network with the Brain as described above. Connecting the ZigBee network to the Internet in this way also opens up the possibilities for remote monitoring the network health, as can be seen in Figure 4, and even issuing a remote reset if needed.

Remote firmware upload

Go for IT! uses the ZigBee network not only for game communication but also for the remote uploading of new firmware and games.

Each location is controlled by an Arduino[4] board. A custom bootloader for the Arduino and a firmware uploader for the host computer is written by the Go for IT! team to make remote programming of the Arduino possible. The firmware uploading can be done directly via the ZigBee network or over the Internet connection via the ZigBee Internet gateway.

Appendix A

User - IVR scheme

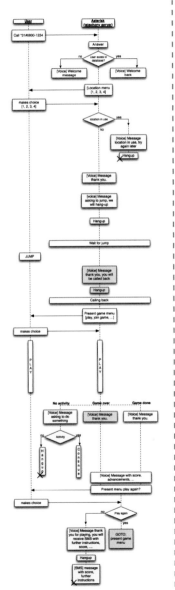

Appendix B

Go for IT! communication flow

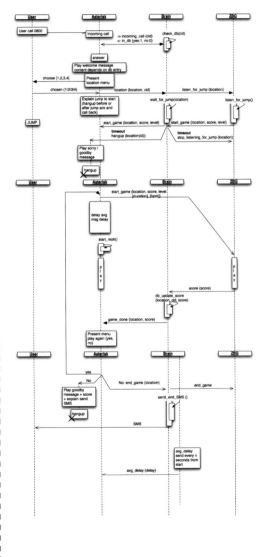

Go for IT!
Hardware
overview

Rene Wassenburg

The custom designed hardware for the go-for-it! game can be found under the pavement at all individual game locations.

This hardware-system contains the actual electronics that run the game software, control the physical layer of the game (the tiles) and communicates with the Brain.
The core of this system is an Arduino Duemilanove.

The entire hardware is powered by a 12VDC / 150W switch mode power supply. This power supply is mounted in the nearest lamppost close to the actual game location. The brand of the power supply is Meanwell, typenr CLG-150-12A. Documentation about this supply can be found here: www.meanwell.com/search/clg-150/default.htm

The Arduino
The Arduino Duemilanove is the heart of the system. This Arduino is equipped with a ATmega328.
- It runs standalone on a 12VDC input
- It runs the game software
- It reads out the piezo inputs (on/off) over a dedicated SPI bus.

The block diagram of the system is the following:

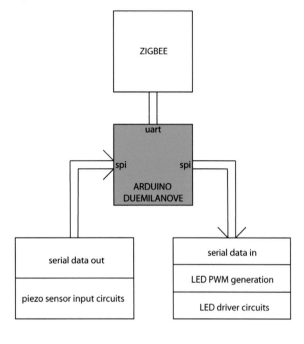

- It controls the LED-outputs by periodically sending (12bit) PWM values for all LEDs over a dedicated SPI bus.
- It communicates with the Brain using the UART, connected to the zigbee controller.

The pinout used in this hardware setup is as following:
- Digital GPIO5: SPI LED clock
- Digital GPIO6: SPI LED data
- Digital GPIO7: SPI LED latch
- Digital GPIO8: SPI PIEZO clock
- Digital GPIO9: SPI PIEZO data
- Digital GPIO10: SPI PIEZO latch
- UART Tx: Zigbee Tx
- UART Rx: Zigbee Rx

Piezo inputs

Each piezo signal enters the circuit via a zener-diode to clamp the signal in between 0-5V. This signal is then being fed into an ultra high gain amplifier stage, followed by a buffer

stage with an added offset to eliminate possible noise. The circuit contains 48 of these stages, so 48 piezos can be connected to the system.

All individual amplier outputs are fed into a 48-channel shift register, to be able to transport the piezo data serially to the Arduino using a dedicated SPI bus.

The output of this stage is fed into an 8-bit shift register (74HC165). In total there are 6 shift registers to be able to read out 48 piezos. For the game only 2x23 inputs are used, leaving 2 inputs unused. The data from the shift registers is transported to Arduino over a dedicated SPI bus.

See following diagrams for a visual representation.
- one piezo input circuit
- daisy chain of all piezo inputs

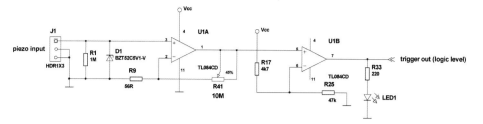

Piezo Input Stage

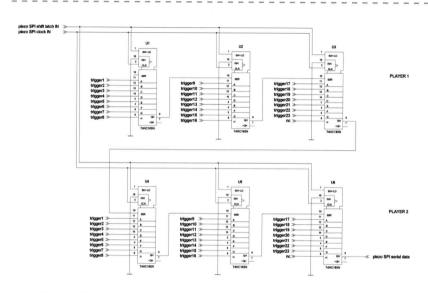

Daisy Chain of Piezo Inputs

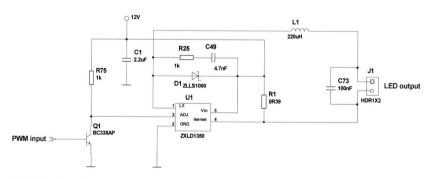

Led Driver Circuit

LED outputs

The LEDs are controlled using a 144 channel 12-bit PWM generator. This generator is controlled by the Arduino using a dedicated SPI bus. Each individual output of this generator is connected to a LED driver. The LED drivers are capable of driving 1W power LEDs.

There are 23 tiles per player field, and there are two player fields per location. Each tile contains three LEDs (R, G, B). This means there are 2x23x3=138 PWM channels and thus 138 LED drivers necessary. For design convenience, this is rounded off to 144 (6 channels not used).

The PWM generator is built up by using six 24-channel PWM controllers. The component chosen for this job is the TLC5947 from TI. Each

LED driver is designed around a ZXLD1350 from Zetex to achieve an average LED current of 260mA at 155kHz. The efficiency at 12V is 85%.

See following diagrams for a visual representation.

- one led driver
- daisy chaining the TLC5947.

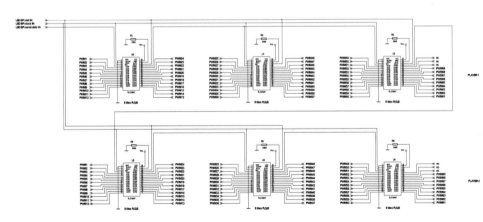

Daisy Chain of Led Outputs

Andreas.
Muk·Haider

Photo essay

117

Go for IT!

Sietse Dols

Go for IT! was originally developed by the 2009 Patching Zone team. During my internship at The Patching Zone over the period of February – June 2010, I contributed to the further concept development of the Go for IT! project.

The design cycle of the concept development was set up so that the advantages of the 2009 game mechanics would be used while minimizing the cons of the 2009 game mechanics.

2009 game mechanics (act out) >> persona's >> (renewed) game mechanics >> Usability research

During the earlier phases of the concept development of the 2010 Go for IT! there was no working Go for IT! platform available. Therefore it was chosen to use the physical brainstorming method 'Acting out'[1] to become familiar with the various concepts and find potential design improvements. The output of the 'Act out' served as input for points of

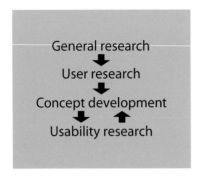

General research
↓
User research
↓
Concept development
↓ ↑
Usability research

Figure 1 Design cycle during the
concept development(diagram)

Figure 2 Jakob Nielsen's Alert box.

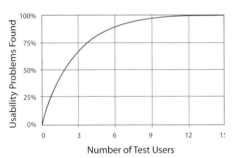

attention during the usability research and also as early inputs for the renewal of the game mechanics.

At the base of the Go for IT! user testing was the personas framework of Cooper.[2] During the research for the personas, Go for IT! was enriched by information from the Big South Lab project. Since both projects had the same target group, the input gained during the workshops of the Big South Lab could be used for the Go for IT! project.

The workshops of the Big South Lab turned out to be a good tool for extensive contact with the target group of youth between 16 years up to 22 years old. The advantage of user research for personas via workshops was that in an informal setting the difficult to reach target group had no direct pressure to discuss their personal interest. But over time, with no pressure, they did discuss their preferences vividly. Moreover in general the contact period during workshops is longer than during interviews. I believe that overall this allowed the participants to extensively and considerately provide the project with useful information.

Furthermore team members of Go for IT! 2009 were interviewed so that I could quickly gain a large amount of information about the target group. Based on user insights gained from these interviews and the Big South workshops personas were setup.

These personas provide a basis for user testing within the Go for IT! project. Since the personas can help communication about the project with other designers and stakeholders. The personas were used to accommodate the target group as far as possible. Since there was only a limited amount of personas compared to the size of the target group, it was easier to discuss the wishes of the various users using personas.

Within the next phase of the concept development a formative evaluation of the game (mechanics) was done. The formative evaluation was based on the literature of Jakob Nielsen[3]. The goal of the usability tests was to gain information about how the Go for IT! was used, what the user likes and dislikes.

The results can be used for further development of the game mechanics. The game was tested by six different people aged between 17 - 23 years old. This amount of participants was chosen based on the Alert box (figure 2). The Alert Box indicates that with six participants 85% of the usability problems can be found. A higher amount of participants would be inefficient time and money.

The results of the user test show that the game in essence is appealing to the target group (especially the lower aged region of the target group). From a design perspective the value that workshops have was proven within this project. I have experienced that the workshops are a good alternative to enquiries and interviews, especially for a difficult to reach target group. Another advantage is that by getting to know your participants, they are often more willing to help you in a later stage for example during the usability research. The downside of opting workshops is that they're time consuming. However in a situation were several projects are running parallel, like the Go for IT! and the Big South Lab, research can be shared and thus time can be saved.

References:
1 Michalko M., Thinkertoys, published by Ten Speed Press, 2006
2 Cooper, R. and Reimann, R., Modeling users: Personas and Goals, 2007
3 Nielsen J., Usability Engineering, published by Morgan Kaufmann, 1994

Pinar Temiz
Interview by Sam Nemeth

Pinar Temiz is a music student at the Hogeschool voor de Kunsten Utrecht and heard about The Patching Zone from a friend. She applied when the call for the Go for IT project was sent out and stayed for 1.5 years in Rotterdam South, also working on the follow up project: Big South.

Can you describe your first experiences at The Patching Zone?

The first days, when I arrived, everybody seemed completely lost. The group literally came from countries all over the world and because of this sudden change of environment, it took people some time to get their bearings. They all moved to the Rotterdam South area where the project was also located.

This has considerable advantages for the project but is also hard on the team, that not only has to start a project from scratch, but has to get settled on top of this.

The group was intimidating to me. As the only Bachelor student. I was confused about the ambiguity, all the possibilities and our responsability to find our way in it. Of course I was aware of the Processpatching idea that you learn through the process and that all this confusion can be a valuable part of the col-laborative cycle.

After my initial period of paralysis I started getting to know the team and was exited by the people I met and later collaborated with.

How did that work out?

It took some time, I still do not know if I found my place then. I experienced it as a constant struggle to articulate what I wanted and what I could contribute to the project. Positioning yourself is hard in such situations. But in terms of experience I learned a lot, figuring out myself, what my talents and ambitions are. I discovered I have more possibilities than I imagined. I have a better understanding of how I want to work, who I want to co-operate with and what I want to do. It added a number of things to my possbility list. The Patching Zone literally broadened my horizon.

You also worked on the follow-up project: Big South Lab.

Yes, but then I was more prepared. I knew you have to do everything yourself, make your own programme and use every ones' abilities and skills. And I saw history repeat itself. I saw the others being dumped into a completely alien situation and hope I was able to give some comfort. It was an interesting period for me because I could observe the project more de-tached compared to the year before.

In retrospect, how do you see the process-patching method in re-lation to the projects you participated in?

I do not know for sure how the method was ap-plied. During the first project, Go-for IT! I had periods where I was totally lost. More team members felt that way, but I have the impres-sion I was the one voicing it more often.

At those moments, I had the feeling that the project needed more guidance. Personalities clashed, as they do in almost every collabora-tion, but there was little or no management to solve these problems. It is entirely possible that this was all part of the 'work in progress'-attitide that The Patching Zone chooses, but for us it was not always pleasant and we felt more or less abandoned at times.

On the other hand, I know these creative proc-esses take energy and I met people that are very talented and skilled and worked together with a wonderful bunch of professionals. Towards the end of the first project the roles were more clearly defined, which helped to approach the project in a more structured way.

The Big South project worked out better in a some respects, although it took some time to move to a new location and get the office or-ganized. Maybe also because it was the same environment (Rotterdam South) as the Go-for-IT project, it did not take me too much time to get settled.

My period at The Patching Zone was interest-ing and taught me a lot, oddly enough for a collaborative project, mostly about myself. I have a much better insight into my talents and motivation and the way I position myself towards others in a professional situation. The Patching Zone is the reason I feel good enough about myself to start my masters this year and that is something positive, no?

Nick van den Berg

Interview by Sam Nemeth

Nick van den Berg is senior project manager at Rotterdam Development Cor- poration (OBR)

I know The Patching Zone very directly, as the idea of Anne Nigten. When we met, she was very active at V2_, The Institute for the Unstable Media, to give the combination of art and science a social meaning in Rotterdam. At that time I worked at an organization, set up to provide the Rotterdam area with glassfiber broadband internet to stimulate social and economic innovation. We offered infrastructure to make it attractive for companies to choose for Rotterdam. One of the idea's that floated above the market was the growing awareness

that 'a creative community' had proved to be the economic motor of innovative city-economics. It was with this backdrop that I felt that Anne was one of the people that understood what direction the city was heading for.

Later Anne asked me to look at one of her new idea's: Processpatching. I considered this an honour, so not long after this, an extensive pack of paper landed on my desk. What she actually did was to present an ambitious system that not only tried to facilitate innovation, it also introduced a method for one of the most challenging issues of our times: the collaboration between culture, science and business.
This lead to a couple of conversations and I got seriously interested the method. I thought; this is exactly what this city needs. The Processpatching method is based on the idea of building bridges to create a fertile innovative climate.
Rotterdam is a young city with a problematic side but also with great potential. But you have to be pro-active and keep on stimulating positive trends. We strongly believe in the potential of a solid cultural climate. But you can only stimulate this climate if you work from practice and from the reality of the street. The Patching Zone combines working with new media and the potential of street culture, this is a powerful mix.

Business often specializes in little niches in the market, The Patching Zone focuses on a broad spectrum. It facilitates bonds and coalitions and makes the co-operation possible between organizations, companies and artists. And it is precisely this function, that is the motor of new business: combining people and introducing them to new technology but also to innovative ideas and new ways of marketing, that makes The Patching Zone unique.
One of the most interesting vantage points of The Patching Zone is to introduce education in a way and on a place where you would normally not find it, and both parties can benefit from this. Education receives input directly through practice and business is opened up to innovative input, from a source that is directly connected with the cultural core of the city and this fact can result in totally different ways of entrepreneurship.

University is still in many ways an introverted institute. This is one of the reasons people with a university-education have difficulties to find a suitable job in a down-to-earth city such as Rotterdam. There is not much connection with what we call 'the street', a mix of people, cultures, businesses, ideas, ideals, sales techniques, religions, music, rhythms, theatre traditions and stories, a body that is steadily growing and exactly the element that makes Rotterdam unique.

If we take a little bit of this mix, this feeling, and give it to the people that help shape business in this town, and if we give the people that embody this community the possibilities to use their identities, to work from their identities, we have reached some of our goals, I think.
It is actually simple: there's a match between business, the people at rock bottom of this society and the educational institutes, and that is the ideal combination and these are the gears that The Patching Zone uses to shift between...

Partners

Ministerie van Onderwijs, Cultuur en Wetenschap

Ministerie van Economische Zaken

AC de Groot bv

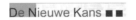
De Nieuwe Kans ■ ■

V2_ institute for the unstable media

virtueel _ platform

kosmopolis rotterdam

Stichting Welzijn Feijenoord

DEEL FEIJEN OORD GEMEENTE

worldteleconnect international

Candelled

Cultuur scouts

CF

Sonor

U
Unilever

Recycle-X

RE-X
reuse + recycle + refactor + remix + redistribute

Recycle-X
January 2010 – September 2010

Commissioners / partners:	Noordkaap Dordrecht
Funders / sponsors:	Trivire, SNS Reaal Fonds, Prins Bernhard Cultuurfonds, Stichting Doen Bank Giro Loterij, VSB Fonds, CCC program run by Dutch Ministry of Economic Affairs and the Dutch Ministry of Education, Culture and Science
Target group:	Inhabitants, entrepreneurs and tourists of the Voorstraat North in Dordrecht
Team:	Javier Busturia Cerezo, Jelle Dekker, Jingni Wang, Ricardo de Oliveira Nascimento
Guests:	Zeljko Blace (HR), Stealth (NL), Gilberto Esparza (MX), Kitchen Budapest (HU), Johannes Brechter (DE)
Mentors and Staff:	Kristina Anderson, Sam Nemeth, Simon de Bakker, Dineke Keemink, Anne Nigten, Wilco Tuinman

Recycle-X seeks to make an artistically critical and sustainable contribution to the redevelopment of the Dordrecht shopping street Voorstraat Noord into a main cultural axis for the city. During Recycle-X, The Patching Zone and Stichting Noordkaap will turn Voorstraat Noord into a temporary laboratory. Fine artists, designers, researchers and students from The Patching Zone will participate. There will be a public programme comprising a series of exhibitions, workshops and interventions at various public locations. Users, residents and visitors of Voorstraat Noord and Dordrecht as well as people from outside the city will be actively involved in elements of the program.

BACKGROUND

Recycle-X derives its added value vis-à-vis existing initiatives, partly from the urban redevelopment process in which the project is entering. After a successful two years of Noordkaap in Voorstraat, we have observed that it has been difficult to arrive at a sustainable plan for the city's cultural axis. A range of initiatives have been reviewed, but few have made a lasting impression. Recycle-X springs from our own motivation; there is no political or commercial agenda behind our project. We are mainly interested in new, sustainable and critical approaches to the improvement of Dordrecht cultural life. So this isn't about top-down urban redevelopment principles but enhancing and diversifying the cultural appeal of the city. We wish to achieve this through a short, intensive collaboration between international talents and local stakeholders.

Recycle-X will transform Voorstraat Noord into a 'Living Lab' and a platform for critical collaboration, exchange, and cultural activities. Recycle-X 'guests' will be selected for their experience working in public space and their ability to create platforms for social encounters and interaction around their work.

Recycle-X will aim for a constructively critical big-city confrontation in Voorstraat Noord. The Patching Zone's approach differs from those of other initiatives because of its independent position, whereby the space between fields, disciplines and academic backgrounds can be used in an optimal way for transdisciplinary creative experiments.

Composition of the project

Recycle-X will be made up of various interventions and workshops that will be linked to each other within a long-running creative research project, which will also give rise to a series of public events. The heart of Recycle-X will consist of:

- The Patching Zone team, who will be based for seven months in a combined living and working space at Voorstraat 183
- Art projects and workshops in the street and around the city, put together by Noordkaap and the participating artists (three interventions and three workshops) and The Patching Zone Recycle-X team (two interventions and one or two workshops).

The project will start in January 2010 with a recycling action by the Recycle-X team, who will furnish the workspace and student living areas with recycled materials and furniture from Dordrecht, together with the supervisors from The Patching Zone. We propose that during the introduction week the stakeholders meet the team and show them around Voorstraat Noord and Dordrecht from their own perspectives; for example, the CBK could show them the exhibitions it has organised so far around the development of Voorstraat Noord, the shopkeepers' association could introduce them to the street's businesspeople, Stichting De Stad could take them on an architectural tour, etc. All this information will be incorporated into an artistic intervention by the Recycle-X team in public space. This intervention will be the first public event and will be followed by the first artist residency, that of Gilberto Esparza. Each artist residency will conclude with a workshop by the Recycle-X team and artists, in, for and with the street.

Programme

We will invite the residents and businesspeople of Voorstraat Noord to a series of workshops on topics such as DIY design and experience processes. Members of the public will work closely with the designers, artists and researchers in The Patching Zone's Voorstraat Noord lab. Five artistic interventions will also be organised in the street during the project. With Recycle Your Street, we aim to generate artistic and cultural expressions around the theme of urban sustainability and encourage critical engagement among residents and users of Voorstraat.

Living Lab 24/7 - ongoing intervention

The team will live and work in a building on or near Voorstraat Noord, which will be set up as the Recycle-X lab, so that a constant dialogue with the residents and local businesspeople can take place. The workspace (lab) will also greatly contribute to understanding of the diverse groups that the street attracts at various times of the day, evening and night, with specific accompanying problems. The 'Living Lab' of the Voorstraat will in principle be 'open' 24 hours a day and seven days a week; The Patching Zone team will live and work there, meaning in principle that something could happen at any time, from a workshop to a design experiment or a playful ecological or social action, etc. The details of this component are difficult to predict, because we wish to preserve the freedom to come up with surprising concepts and expressions together with the people of Dordrecht.

The Recycle-X team's work will be anchored in a series of workshops; together with a workshop leader, they will tackle intellectual, artistic and practical urban design problems. They will then elaborate or design projects together with local residents, businesses and passers-by. The brief description below will serve as a guideline for these workshops. Finally, Noordkaap will invite several artists to carry out interventions in the street and in central Dordrecht. The team will work closely with these artists at Noordkaap. The Recycle-X team's role will therefore effectively complement that of the selected artists. The team's assignments will contain plenty of room for surprises and spontaneous interactions with residents, businesspeople and tourists in Voorstraat Noord and the surrounding area. The interventions will be placed in a broader context, because the Recycle-X team will link them to each other and to events taking place elsewhere in the city

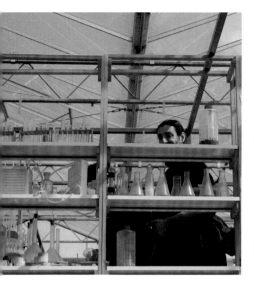

and the world. The team will conclude their programme of activities with a presentation of the results of Living Lab Voorstraat Noord, which will serve as a contribution to the development of the cultural axis. Dordrecht's urban experts will naturally be invited so that a thorough transfer of knowledge can take place and the activities will take on a sustainable character.

We will invite the residents and businesspeople of Voorstraat Noord to workshops on do-it-yourself design processes. Prototypes for sustainable urban development concepts will be developed here. Residents and users of the street will be invited to two artist-led workshops, in which future scenarios for the street will be constructed.

How was Recycle-X developed?

As detailed above the Recycle-X project was anchored in a series of encounters with visiting artists and local events. In that way, the ongoing work by the team was reinforced by the meetings with Gilberto Esparza, the Urban Explorer festival, and Kitchen Budapest.

While the team continued to be engaged in the overall work of defining what sustainable living could mean within a Voorstraat context, there was a clear progression of thematic work through the whole period. In that sense the overall themes read like this: light, water, growing, cooking, sewing, distibution and repurposing. Each of these themes manifested itself in either a workshop, investigation or public event. The Recycle-X work then follows both a progression and maturation of ideas and an important seasonnal narrative, starting with a dark January where light becomes a primary concern, moving through the growing season towards a point where a warm and sunny Dordrecht lends itself to sharing and distribution of both food and ideas. Another factor in the period was the process of the team becoming 'at home' in the street and the various social networks that operate around it. Toward the end of the project the team wrote a one week organic-living diary that clearly illustrates this process of finding and connecting with local networks.

The last piece in this series of work will be a publication that distills these experiences into a small instruction manual. The manual will be distributed locally with the idea that the continuation of the Recycle-X work is now in the hands of the Voorstraat itself.

What if we can decon-
struct people's way
to feel the world,
how would the world
be?

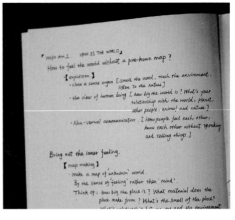

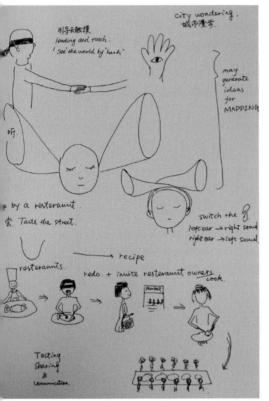

My mind goes to the sens-
ing directly: what if we
could only feel the world
by touching and tasting?
And because the theme is
related to 'expedition', so
'sensing the world by different kinds of body part'
becomes the main point in
my drawing book. I ask myself: how to give people a
chance to feel the world
more by heart rather than
mind?

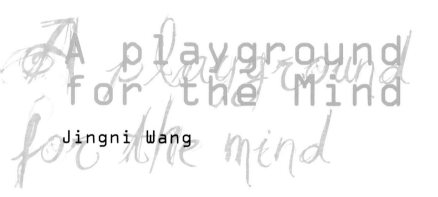

A playground for the Mind

Jingni Wang

I like to draw, because sometimes my mouth is just not enough to express myself well. In English or in general? So, when my mind has something to say, I lay on my bed or on the floor, with my sketch book, and music in the air. In March 2010, we got the chance to do an expedition as a group during Urban Explorers Festival. When we started to think about an expedition of the Voorstraat, I came up with the 'map' idea. The following, are the sketches I made during the process of making the 'Achterstraat' installation for the festival.

In the very beginning, there was not much of an idea, just wondering, strongly wondering.

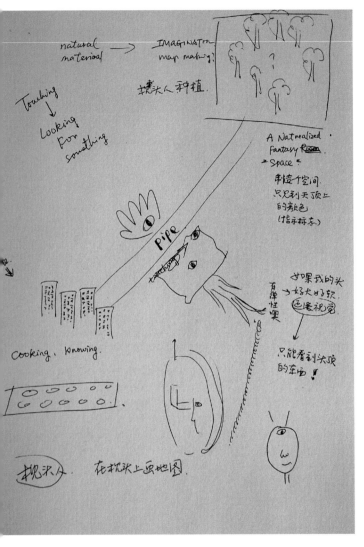

natural material → IMAGINATION map making?

Touching
↓
Looking for something

挖头人 种植.

A Naturalized Fantasy Room = Space =
半造一个空间.
只尼到天顶上
的颜色
(指示标志)

pipe
touch point

如果我的头
→ 好大好软
造虚视觉
有弹性奥

只能看到头顶
的东西!

Cooking, knowing.

挖头人.   在挖头上画地图.

Then, pick-ing up the main points of each team member, ear, sound, se-cret, fabric, became the key words of the map of voor-straat. In or-der to explain what kind of sound I am in-terested in, I drew this pic-ture.

moving ear

Then, after a week of think-ing, we started to talk, and our team mem-bers feel that 'secrets of the voorstraat is a interest-ing topic, and somehow, I drew this picture.

Finally, our team make a conclusion, and made the installation 'Achterstraat' as described:

The Achterstraat is the part of the street you normally don't see, don't hear and don't know. In this project we evoke people to explore hidden parts of the street, but we also share their and others secrets. Spread around a part of the Voorstraat you will find ears. In these ears you can whisper you secrets, stories or gossip, or fragments of sound from the street. In the 'Achterstraat HQ' at Voorstraat 183 you can explore the textile map to bring these recordings back to life. You might hear what's going on there now, what you told before or other secrets and stories shared by others.

The map of the street is made in a patchwork way from textiles in collaboration with the Recycle-X neighbours 'Wereldwijven' The textiles, embroidery sound and smells in the map bring a whole new view on and representation of the street.

It's a part
of map.

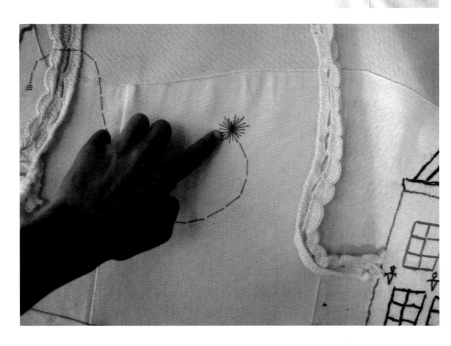

The start shape point is the button of sound, when
you touch it, you open it.

Ladies working on the map.

Craft and Technology

Ricardo Nascimento

Keywords:
Craft
Technology
Flexible circuitry
Community
Street
Secrets
Interactivity
Tangible interface

I would like to present in this text the production background of the interactive installation 'Achterstraat' that was developed by the Recycle-X team together with Noordkaap and commissioned by the Urban Explorer Festival 2010[1]. Through the use of embroidery techniques, smart materials and digital audio processing we created a piece that aimed to reflect and reveal an unusual side of the Voorstraat in Dordrecht (Netherlands). A piece about the street, made by the street.

Introduction

One of the main axes of Recycle-X activities is to try to (re)integrate people that live and use the Voorstraat. With this idea in mind we developed the interactive installation 'Achterstraat'.
This piece aims to represent the part of the street you don't normally see, hear or notice. In this project we invited people to explore hidden parts of the street and anonymously share se-

1   www.urbanexplorers.nl

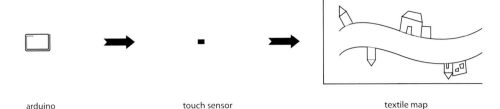

arduino   touch sensor   textile map

Figure 2
Interaction system.

Figure 3
Member of Recycle-X drawing the building's façade.

crets and thoughts. We thought that this spontaneous information collected from passers-by and from the residents could reveal a bit more about the personality of the street and in doing so, contribute to the understanding of its functions and dynamics. Another interesting aspect for us was that people would recognize themselves in this project as part of the street. Using the street, people could give life and meaning to it and 'Achterstraat' tries to represent this idea in a tangible way.

Functioning
Spread around on the north part of the Voorstraat we fixed six silicon ears embedded with a pre-amplified microphone (see figure 1). These microphones were connected via cable to an audio interface[2] that was connected to a computer running MAX/MSP[3]. The computer was then connected to an Arduino microcontroller[4] that makes the interface with the physical textile map of the street through touch sensors[5] (see figure 2). The touch sensors are attached to the map via a conductive thread embroidered onto the fabric. When someone touched the embroidery, it activated the touch sensor and triggered the sound collected by the microphone network and recorded by the computer system. A speaker behind the fabric would broadcast the sound.

2   Focusrite Saffire PRO 10 I/O 8-channel Mic Preamp with FireWire interface.
3   Max/MSP is a visual programming language for music and multimedia. More information at www.cycling74.com
4   Arduino is an open-source electronics prototyping platform based on flexible, easy-to-use hardware and software. It's intended for artists, designers, hobbyists, and anyone interested in creating interactive objects or environments. (www.arduino.cc)
5   We use the sensor QT 113 from Quantum research Group. The QT113 charge-transfer ('QT') touch sensor is a self-contained digital IC capable of detecting near-proximity or touch.

Figure 4
Building's facade

Design Process

We had about one month to produce the piece and in order to accomplish it we decided to ask for help. Together with the Urban Explorer Festival Organization we put an advertisement in the local newspaper asking for volunteers to help us embroider the map and in return we would give free passes to the festival. Besides this action we worked together with Wereldwijven[6], an association that works mainly with migrant ladies and produces several kinds of handwork. They are extremely good in a variety of crafts and we thought it would be great to have their style on the map. Also the fact that this is a multicultural organization could give a nice mix to the project. At first the Recycle-X team went out to the street to draw the building's facade on paper (see figure 3). As we had to cable all the microphones we had a limitation on the area, so we decided to make the map only about 100 meters to the south of our house (Voorstraat 183) and 100 meters to the north. The drawings ended up having five different styles. After we drew the facades we transferred them to a semi transparent paper in the size of the final map. Next, the drawings were handed to volunteers who started to embroider them onto pieces of fabric that would be put together afterwards (see figure 4 and 5).

We decided to leave the aesthetic decisions for each of the contributors, including the color pallet and embroidery technique. This created a nice variety of styles that actually reflected the diversity of the people who have a connection with the street (see figure 6). This decision was

6   http://www.wereldwijven.info/

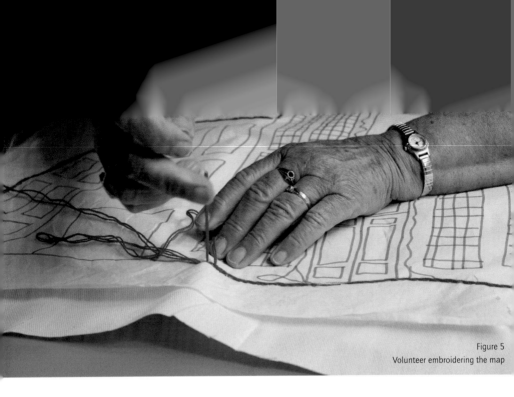

Figure 5
Volunteer embroidering the map

made in order to give the volunteers a certain ownership. It turned out to be a good decision, when the participants could easily see themselves in the work they identified with the piece.

They choose a color palette together (orange, pink, yellow and red) and the technique was up to each of them. Some buildings ended up very simple and minimalist and others quite complex and detailed. After every individual facade was embroidered, Jingni from the Recycle-X team sewed them together. We noticed that some parts of the map remained a bit empty and to improve it we started to do some collage, adding flowers, animals and people made out of textiles.

The handwork was finished at the very last minute and this collaboration was one the strongest aspects of the work where women and men worked together to complete the work. During the last days we worked in our space so passers-by could see our 'work in progress', this experience was very stimulating. During the process of making we could chat, talk about the street and get to know each other better, we really had the feeling that we put our efforts together to create a common piece. The fact that we were working together on the piece created common issues amongst us and allowed people on the street to act and behave as a community.

Technology and Interaction

The interactivity of the piece was developed by the Recycle-X team. To connect the sensors to the map we used 'smart materials' like conductive thread and conductive fabric. Through the use of these materials we could connect the map to the computer with a touch sensor and an Arduino board.

Figure 6
Final map

The conductive thread was embroidered on the map in the same location where the ears were placed. The use of thread to create the interaction did not affect the aesthetic of the map and allowed the use of technology in a non-obtrusive way. For the people who interacted with the piece it looked like a big craftwork. The fact it was interactive was an unexpected behavior of the map (see figure 7).

On the technological side of the work, we recorded the sounds coming from the microphones in Max/Msp for 5 seconds, the last recorded sound was reproduced every time someone touched the map on the places embroidered with the conductive thread. So, in order to hear what was recorded on an ear placed in a specific location on the street, you should touch the embroidery at this same location. To decide when to record a sound we created a threshold in Max/Msp. When the level of noise was above the threshold the system started to record and when the level of noise was below the threshold the system just ignored the sound.

We had some problems with noise from the microphones, which distorted the in Max/Msp recording threshold and resulted in unintended sound recordings. Our troubleshooting showed that this was due to the long cables and high battery consumption. After the second day some of the microphones did not work at all. Also the multichannel equipment started to have strange and unpredictable behavior in communication with MAX/MSP. The equipment sometimes ignored channels and needed to be restarted to work properly again. Because of this the installation was under maintenance for some moments during the exhibition.

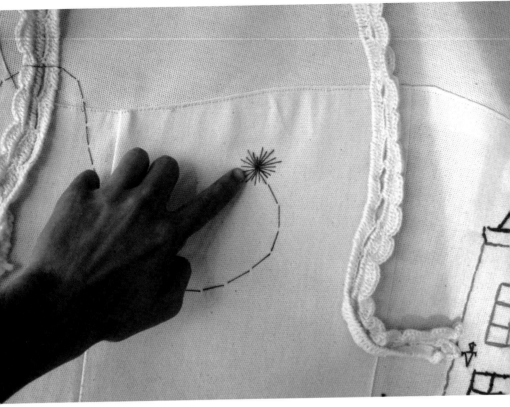

Figure 7
Embroider with conductive thread. Touching this part you activate
the sound

Conclusion

During the 3 days of the festival the installation was visited by lots of people and we had good feedback from the public and curators. Most of the visitors liked very much the map and its style and were amazed by the possibility to hear the street sounds in a different way.

Many of the volunteers who helped to make the map came during the festival to see the final results and they seemed proud of their work.

From the technical problems, we learned for an installation of that magnitude of complexity, involving long cables and lots of different equipment and sensor technology, one needs at least one week to test the interactive system and to correct possible bugs. Also, we could try to use a more stable wireless microphone system. This option was initially put aside due to the high cost of renting but it would have made the system more stable and free from noise. Another operational aspect that we could avoid by using the wireless microphones is the task of collecting the wired microphones at the end of every day whilst leaving the cables on the street. Fortunately no one stole them but this was a possibility we needed to consider when working with art installations in public space. Despite these unexpected technical problems the piece was successful and enjoyable, but what was more important for us was that through it we could reinforce a sense of community and bring people together that in any other situation would not happen.

The combination of craft, smart materials and sensor technology turned out to be a very effective way to present an interactive piece for an audience that is not familiar with this kind of work. Normally, interactive installations have this aura of something extremely high tech and complex. When we combined this with these traditional techniques we put the piece closer to something that people were used to and thus we created empathy.

This project also made the relation between Recycle-X and the neighbors stronger and gave us visibility on the street. This was really nice and after that we had much more help in other projects developed by our team.

Javier Busturia

Interview by Kristina Andersen

How does collaboration fit into your own work and process. What is the role of 'others' in your work?

When the collaboration concept comes to my mind I always think in a horizontal way of working. What does it mean? Exactly that, you are on the same level as the other people you are working with. The history of the arts shows us how the role of the artist has been egocentric ("The true artist helps the world by revealing mystic truths" Bruce Nauman). But there have always been some who had other concerns, and tried to work in an 'expanded field'. Artists can work together to produce art, but so can scientists, philosophers, sociologists or any other person. Joseph Beuys talked about this; everyone is an artist. What he wanted to say in my opinion is that anyone has the potentiality to use the human tool of creativity. This is then collaboration for me, to open your mind and be prepared for this spontane-

ity with others. In Recycle-X collaboration has been a key concept for all of our work. From the beginning we wanted to build bridges with the local people in our context: our neighbours in the Voorstraat, the shop owners, the local artist community and organisations like the Couch Surfers and Transition Town.

A good example is the project with Gilberto Esparza, Plantas Parlantes which was completely developed in a collaborative way. At the beginning of the project we just knew we wanted to work with water and energy. So we started our research: We looked for water specialists, water management educators, architects, gardeners and scientists (who where researching bacteria and plant roots as source of energy), in order to build our project. They didn't work as artists for the project, but their information was crucial for the project. They were pivotal points in the development of the project. Without those conversations we would have done something else.

In my own work I see collaboration as an opportunity to produce richness. Normally, when working alone as an artist, I can bring out all my reflections and personal opinions on an issue. But working together is a way of building small utopias where a temporary horizontal society can appear. Working together is an opportunity for the building of real situations of democracy, in the real meaning of the word.

For me then, art means the possibility to create together. It is a way of expanding my personal world. Last year I had the opportunity to visit an exhibition of Paul Thek, an artist from New York, who was very active during the 60's and

70's. His solo works are very good but the best aspect of his work his ability to put together collaborative artist works; by inviting friends to work in a collective environment. The works were probably done in one afternoon of deep concentration, you can feel that the works are made by different people with different backgrounds and views. You feel a real collaboration going on!

So when Beuys said "everyone is an artist" do you think he meant, that everyone is an artist in their everyday life, or that everyone needs to 'execute art' in a particular setting or a particular situation?
Art is not just something made for the galleries. I don't believe in art like that. For me art is something for the everyday, alive and related to us as thinking animals, animals who have the capacity of reflection and representation. Art helps you to understand the world. As the slogan of the alternative Spanish Sevilla Bienal (BIACS) in 2006 declared: ¡Arte todos los días! (art everyday!). I don't feel that Beuys thought that art is something meant for

special locations or situations. It is something powerful that can happen between people. The only requirement is that you must be conscious that you are having a creative moment.

I think that Beuys meant that everyone has the opportunity to produce changes, that the potential to create and produce changes is part of being human. We are animals 'programmed' to change. Art is a tool, as any other human tool, but fed from creativity and personal reflections. We can use it in our daily life or in a particular case where we decide to produce art. Art can be used as a daily tool, we don't have to be worried about producing final art works every time. I think is more interesting to be open to experiments.

But, let's change the roles... what does collaboration mean for you Kristina, do you see it also as an opportunity or as a problem? Do you think it is possible to work together with people who are not artists, or will the figure of the artist always appear over the work in a collective production?

I normally get out of this conundrum by thinking of the work as 'making'. For me 'making' is a space in which people can meet and bring new things/ insights and strategies into existence. I am very interested in this meeting of minds and hands. As far as I am concerned it makes no real difference if people self-identify as artists or not, artists are not always the most open and interesting people I meet.

Actually, I think most artists have problems with the need to be recognized. In the art world it is very important to build a label: Artist, with your name close to it. If you manage to build your label and be recognized, you will become a brand. I think, we focus too much in the individual person, and I think that this makes it impossible to continue to create change. It stops us from taking risks and it means that we can only produce change in the form of products. Art ought to be an experiment always. And if we have this idea clear in our minds, we can break down the barriers that prevent us from learning from the other individuals we are working with, from the collective itself, from the collective mind.

What are the charac-
teristics of a suc-
cessful collabora-
tion? What attitudes
and qualities must be
there? How can it be
supported?

I think real collaboration only happens, when you forget your interests and personal goals. Instead of that you focus on the goal of the collective, you work for this and you become something else that is not only your individual self. When I work in a collective I try to forget my previous work and focus on what is wanted at this time, what the group is searching for. I will feed the group with my interests and background, but not the other way around. If someone in the group forgets this and works thinking about his/her own profit, the group product will clearly be damaged, and of course that person will finish leaving the project be-cause it can never perfectly fit an individuals goals.

To work together is very difficult. Really, I don't think it is easy. Only people prepared to build together can do it, it is not something that all artists can do! First one must have an aperture to other's work and interests. Then you need to be focused on listening what the others want to tell you. You must know how to share tasks, how to be ready for dialogue, and really impor-tant, keep always in mind a horizontal way of relating to others. There is no room for author-ity here.
Collaboration means to work together on a concrete objective. That's it, forget the rest! Be open to learn, be open for spontaneity.

Conversely: What will
break a collaboration?
When this occurs is very hard for the group, but

Tatlin wrote in 1919 "the individual is the collector of the energy of the collective, an energy directed towards both knowledge and invention. The initiative individual serves as a contact between the invention and the creativity of the collective". For me that means that the artists can feed with the collective work with their abilities, not lead the work. Collaboration should flow, and the artist should function as a catalyst of the experience.

How do you think we can create collaborative environments for other people?

I guess it has something to do with both culture and education. If you want people to collaborate, you need to look for people with an open mind and open interests. If artists are too focused in their way of working, probably they will work better alone than in a group. Also what you can provide is a good environment for collaboration, which for me means: help on facilitating connections, introductions to interesting external professionals, facilitating the process of working together. An initial theme for the work could be also provided, this will attract people who are already interested in the subject and then it will be easier to start the collaboration.

it sometimes happens. A collaboration is broken when someone is feeling more important than the others, when such a person works to increase his or her importance and takes more power than the rest. These are the common problems of organized social groups. Authority is a problem if people don't know how to deal with it. Collaborative projects should be lead by group decisions and horizontal relations. When the balance is lost, the problems start. When we forget the goal of the group or when we forget to leave space for spontaneity, collaboration is no longer happening.

For us at Recycle-X the theme of the work was already there, and it was quite open (recyclism). The individual interest and backgrounds of the involved participants in the team created an interpretation of the concept in one direction and not in others. We shared our individualities in order to know which path to take as a collective.

When we work with people who do not self identify as artist, it is important to build a good open and collaborative environment where the artist initiate the connections, and in this way facilitate others. You should be able as an artist to be sharp and ambitious in your work, and at the same time modest and horizontal enough to make the collaboration flow.

> Tell me a bit more about, how the collaboration with Gilberto Esparza on the Plantas Parlantes project worked out

Gilberto is used to work with people from both the arts and other fields, industrial designers, engineers, scientists and university staff. He is so focused on making the work happen that his own research transforms itself into a group research. People collaborate with him because they share the interest and because of the way the work flows. When he arrived in Dordrecht it was also like this. We knew some months before that we were going to work with him, so we were prepared for his arrival. By that time at the beginning of the project, we were working on energy experiments, looking for alternative energy from solar panels and fruits, inspired by the Argentinean artist Víctor Grippo (1936-2002) who worked with energy from potatoes. We also had a strong desire to work with plants and people, connecting them in any way possible. We were growing our first seedlings and making an urban garden in our work/home. It was funny when Gilberto came and saw what we were doing in our garden. We immediately knew that we had synergy to make a common project. He wanted to do something with his

ongoing research on energy from bacteria, taking a step further and using plants. He needed water for making his machine work through bacterial activity, and we wanted to work with urban gardening and alternative energies, so the mix was perfect.

At the beginning we were looking for places in Dordrecht where we could collect polluted water from organic waste, but this country seems to be a paradise for keeping water clean. We met people from Weizigt NMC in Dordrecht, an educational centre for sustainability; Henk Ketelaars from Waterschap Hollandse Delta, specialized on treatment of the local drinkable

water; Frans den Houter, architect specialized in sustainable architecture, who knows a lot about Dordrecht and its water. After these meetings we realised that water wasn't organically polluted in Dordrecht. All these meetings were crucial for the developing of the project and direction of strategies.

I feel that collaboration with Gilberto was easy and productive because the common interest and the open minds of the people working together. He could have taken a directing role, as he was the invited artist. But I feel we were working at the same level, with the same level of decisions, always discussing what direction should be taken in order for everyone to be satisfied. The creative atmosphere was so strong with him, it was for sure one of the high points of the Recycle-X project. This only happens when the collective surge above the individuality.

This makes me think:
Do you think we can
collaborate with
nature?

Well. That might sound crazy to most of the people, but actually I think humans have been doing it from the beginning! The animals that today we consider domestic, were transformed from wild ones by human selection and the use of their resources. The seeds that we plant and consume are evolved in exactly the same way. The honey might be a more clear example: by taking care of bee colonies we get their products: honey and wax. The collaboration is there. I think that is not crazy to think about collaboration possibilities with nature in art production, done in a way so artist doesn't take

undue advantage of nature, and tries to learn more from it. It is interesting to place yourself at the same level of a plant for the process of producing a work. And actually this was our position for Plantas Parlantes.

I think this is an ongoing subject for the arts, and I think we will get lot of answers in the next few years. It is difficult in the sense that it is not possible to communicate with nature in the way that we do with other humans, we must find other ways or other tools. It is difficult to know if Nature is interested in producing artworks together with us! But for sure it is possible to produce works that might interest Nature, like the ones that point to solutions for both landscape-environment and humans at the same time. We are part of the planet, we don't own it, so it is a very interesting idea to think and make work about!

Lights and probes

Jelle Dekker

Recycle-X seeks to make an artistically critical and sustainable contribution to the redevelopment of the Dordrecht shopping street Voorstraat Noord into a main cultural axis for the city. During Recycle-X, The Patching Zone and Stichting Noordkaap will turn Voorstraat Noord into a temporary laboratory. Users, residents and visitors of Voorstraat Noord and Dordrecht as well as people from outside the city will be actively involved in elements of the program.

I participated in the Recycle-X project as an intern during my studies at Technical University, Eindhoven. During my internship (January - June 2010), Recycle-X has made several large projects together with different partners and people from the local community. For me it was important in the project to develop different designs for the specific context and situation in Voorstraat Noord. Combining the strength of people from different backgrounds and cultures (other team members and the local community) to come to designs which evoke (playful) inter-action in public space using a relevant connection between the digital and tangible world.

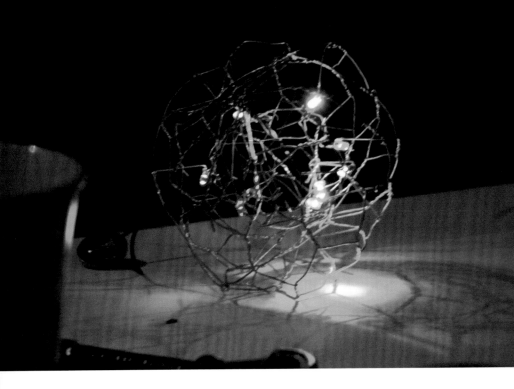

In the following text I will describe two of the participatory actions we undertook at the start of the year, the light workshops and the cultural probe.

The Light Workshop(s)

Intro

What can you do with the street and its lights? What can you do in Recycle-X to discuss it or to design together? These were the questions that Recycle-X was asking at the start of the project for the design of the first workshops. We wanted to know how we could use technology which is very familiar to us, like LED's and batteries, but not well known to most therefore a good starting point to engage people in a workshop to create something new. The starting point for working with lights was that we heard many local people complaining about the December lights put up by the city each year.

In the workshops the participants got to work with pictures and chalk to draw and design, this was followed by connecting the LED's and batteries to make their own lights. The first workshop was aimed at children and used as a warm up since it was the first event by the group and our first experience of giving a workshop together. The second light workshop was aimed at shop owners and other locals from the street and went a bit deeper into the technical aspects and we discussed issues and ideas about lighting in public space.

Preparation & Promotion

For the lights workshops the Recycle-X team organised everything; preparation included not only the technical aspects and content but also the promotion to get the project known locally and to invite people to participate in the workshops.

Photos from the street were printed in black and white as a canvas to work on, this was done so that people had a starting point for drawing pubic lights instead of having to start from nowhere on a blank canvas. For the construction of the lights two choices were made. For the children it would be 'throwies' (led taped onto battery) to stick through the drawing. The system for the other workshop consisted of two layers of chicken wire in between which the LED's were placed and one layer connected to the plus of the battery (or other power source) and the other to the minus. The chicken wire replaces normal wiring and allows participants make a sculpture out of the circuit without the need for soldering.

For the promotion, posters and subscription cards were made and distributed to several locations, including local shops and the local museum and music school. To make the posters a font was used from text found in the street, these special fonts made the posters recognisable and part of the street and the project. Here Recycle-X first encountered how hard it can be to get the locals (and especially the shop owners) to join in or display the poster. This in contradiction to the cultural organisations (Pictura, Music School) and other communities (CouchSurfers) who were much more open to the concept.

It also turned out, especially with the first workshop for the children, to be hard to predict how many people would come. For this first workshops a lot of people took the subscription cards from the posters, but never came.

Results & Response

The light workshops proved to be difficult to organise especially looking at the promotion and getting people to join in. With the first workshop aimed at children it was necessary to pick up some children from the street at the very last moment, promotion through the music school apparently was not enough. In the end though the children who did come had a nice afternoon and went home proud with the new lights they had made themselves.

The second workshop featured the same drawing with chalk onto the street image to get people to think about public lights, but it continued not with throwies but with a lesson on connecting LED's to the chicken wire and the power source. Interestingly people really started to think of the shapes and sculptures they wanted to make into a light and in the end they went home just as proud of their creations as the children before. Also the participants understood how to make the lights but the working of the LED's with the simple connection to the battery did not loose it's magic.. For my own tests before the workshop I also made a larger setup with the RE-X letters all lit up in sequence using an Arduino as power supply. It's that easy to make your own light emitting advertisement.

The Cultural Probe

For the Recycle-X project I wanted to do a cultural probe as a method to get information and participation from the local community over a longer period of time than with a survey or interview. The participants were given a diary with one page per day, some postcards with questions inserted and a camera with the request to take different pictures of the street or things from elsewhere that you would like to have in the street.

In the early phase of the Recycle-X project the interest lay mostly on getting to know the residents in the Voorstraat, what made the Voorstraat different to other streets in Dordrecht and what made it the way it is today. Because a cultural probe takes some effort from the participants, they were handed out after the light workshop to the people who wanted to join in. Even so only two out of five probes returned of which only one person had made an effort.

Combining the info from the cultural probe and the interviews and talks with locals in this particular part of the Voorstraat, there was quite a large group of shop owners and artists who try to make something out of the street. However they do not represent the whole street and don't share the opinions of the city council. I.e. they can't change anything on the actual street because of the parking places that need to stay.

At the start of the project I set myself the following goal: "Can we use the knowledge, input and identity of the local community to make a design that can 'improve' the neighbourhood by invoking more (playful) interaction in the public space. And can I translate this into something that (with adaptations) could fit more of these areas to make the streets more enjoyable. Important for this design is that it's something that can be sustained by the local community and contains an element of recycling of energy or other resources."

Now I would conclude that back then I was looking far too much at this project as a regular TU/ Eindhoven project, which it wasn't. The project consisted of many different projects and collaborations and not so much in one dominant direction. To answer the original question I would say that there is not one design to solve a 'problem' as with this street, to get the liveliness and atmosphere in the street that is wanted you need to get away from the top-down approach and get people to collaborate. A design of (an object for) the street can be a starting point, but if the locals are not involved enough in (co)-designing it will not be 'theirs' enough.

Partners

 Ministerie van Onderwijs, Cultuur en Wetenschap

Ministerie van Economische Zaken

SNS REAAL Fonds

STICHTING DOEN

BankGiro Loterij

 Tr(v(re wonen

Prins Bernhard Cultuurfonds

 VSBfonds

Big South Lab
January 2009 - December 2009
Status: work in progress

Commissioners / funders:	Rotterdam South Pact, CCC programme by the Dutch Ministry of Economic affairs and the Dutch Ministry of Education, Culture and Science
Partners:	Kosmopolis Rotterdam, SWF youth workers, Frequency Foundation, Nieuwe Kans, SBAW, Borough of Feijenoord
Target group:	local youth 15-27
Genre:	media training and multimedia production
Team:	Andreas Zingerle, Chris Baronavski, Georgios Papadakis, Pinar Temiz, Sietse Dols, Yening Jin, Eric Parren
Guest:	Tyler Freeman (US)
Work experience team-members:	Kevin Brito, Geoffrey Frimpong, Jay Janga aka Big Jay
Mentors and staff:	Sam Nemeth, Simon de Bakker, Rene Wassenburg, Jaap Bugter, Kristina Andersen, Dineke Keemink, Anne Nigten

Mission

The Patching Zone gained extensive experience, reached numerous young people, and achieved collaboration in the 2009 Go for IT! project in Rotterdam South (Feijenoord borough). During this process, we took inventory of the wishes and needs of our local partners. This has made it clear that there is a strong demand for media technology skills at different levels, particularly among young people. In preparation for the labour market, young people wish to acquaint themselves with creative processes in the areas of video, audio, gaming, graphic techniques and specialised hardware (sensors and actuators). Access to expert knowledge and equipment, and understanding of entrepreneurship are important factors. On the basis of this, we seek to develop the Big South/Groot Zuid project for young people between the ages of 15 and 27, which will be centred on

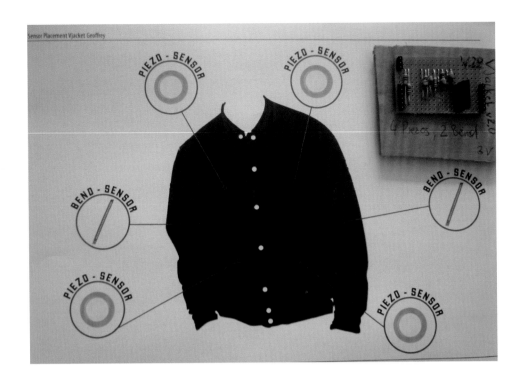

creative entrepreneurship and all its facets. The project will consist of two parts: a Living Lab, where young people can gain experience with creative digital media applications as well as strong theoretical and practical preparation for cultural and social entrepreneurship. In this document, we will describe these two elements, our approach for realising them, and the planned outcomes. Along the way, it will become clear that our approach will provide an initial impulse for the development of an extensive creative-cultural network and a foundation for an innovative creative industry in Rotterdam South.

Geography/reach

In the first year (2010), Big South will work mainly out of Feijenoord and the neighbouring boroughs and make connections with similar initiatives and situations at the national and international (European) level via the Internet. In the subsequent years (2011–2014), we plan to cover all of Rotterdam South and to continue making connections with similar initiatives and situations nationally and internationally (worldwide) via the Internet.

How will Big South distinguish itself?

Big South, executed and initiated by The Patching Zone and its partners, will distinguish itself from competitors and other initiatives through its way of working: above-average students and young professionals will address a single socially relevant project as a team. In addition, The Patching Zone's starting point will be partnership, collaboration between sectors, giving rise to a whole that looks over the boundaries of disciplines. This will be expressed in:

The approach

The Patching Zone will work according to the principle of participatory design. This means that stakeholders (young people/residents) will play an important role in the design, realisation and distribution process. Their roles will vary: designers, usability testers, interns, trend watchers, co-owners of projects. In contrast to the familiar 1970s community-art model, negotiation and collaboration will be central at The Patching Zone; thus for example, much work will be done in processes of exchange and peer-to-peer learning processes.

For the development of Big South (Groot Zuid), The Patching Zone will use the Processpatching approach – developed by initiator Anne Nigten – as a creative research and development method. In it, techniques, methods and knowledge from relevant disciplines and spheres are connected and (re)mixed, giving rise to surprising results that are more than the sum of their parts. Processpatching is especially ideally suited for complex social problems, such as we see in Rotterdam South, because it is custom-made: it uses different perspectives and approaches to construct an individual work model for every situation.

Goals

Primary

The primary goal of Big South is to increase opportunities for young people in Rotterdam South on the creative labour market. We will encourage and train young people whose chances are

'Creative, cultural, social, spatial value, sustainability'

currently slim (and whose motivation is thus often low) with respect to creative entrepreneurship. With our partners (neighbourhood centres, youth workers, social workers and the talent development agency), we will offer talented young people and early school leavers the possibility of preparing for creative entrepreneurship and other places on the job market.

Two important factors will be the learning of skills in disciplines that connect to youth culture and the embedding of learning processes in collaborations between The Patching Zone and local partners. Emphasis will be placed on the peer-to-peer learning process: knowledge acquired in the group will be immediately shared. Thus, a symbiotic structure will arise in which exchange is central and young people gain knowledge and skills at different levels.

Secondary

The secondary goal will be to draw attention to indirect earning models in cultural and social entrepreneurship. In addition to monetary revenues, other factors operating in social, creative and cultural entrepreneurship can indirectly create earning models. These include values that cannot be directly expressed in monetary terms but can have radically positive effects on a neighbourhood: creative value, cultural value, social value, spatial value, sustainability, and exchange of services. Those who recognise and know how to use such values can build a cultural network with a high degree of participation. Such a structure can play a sustainable, positive role.

Digital facility and living lab

The aforementioned goals will be realised through the establishment of a digital facility in one of the neighbourhood centres in South. This digital production facility, or digital lab, will of course benefit from a sustainable approach and require optimal grounding in the local context. To this end, we are already working closely with supervisors at a few neighbourhood centres so that after 2010 the digital lab can be transferred to De Dam or 't Eiland neighbourhood centres and run by staff or volunteers there.

In addition, we will strive for a model in which young people learn from each other and the concepts of expert and amateur are reversed from time to time. With our partners, we are developing an activity programme for the first year according to the so-called Living Lab principle.

The Living Lab is an internationally known user-research facility concept, in which cultural entrepreneurs, small creative businesses and researchers work with knowledge institutes to quickly develop innovative social and cultural productions, products, services and events. The idea of the Living Lab springs from the software and hardware industries. In technology development, the users traditionally enter the picture only after the production phase; in a Living Lab, users are directly involved in the design phase.

Young people, residents and entrepreneurs from the neighbourhood will take part in developing events and productions at an early stage and set up new forms of 'networked' entrepreneurship. Living Labs around the world are connected via the Internet and share knowledge, designs, ideas and thoughts. The Rotterdam South Living Lab will be part of the international Living Lab network and will be housed in the digital production lab, where young people will be able to realise

their own cultural productions (guided by and in close collaboration with the youth workers and The Patching Zone) on an ongoing basis.

The neighbourhood centre will thus involve itself in contemporary youth culture, which makes ever-increasing use of digital media. To provide a starting point as well as a concrete result in the first year of the project, we will present a series of workshops for young people and a joint cross-media event (a game or an exhibition) that will highlight the interwovenness of the virtual and the physical, the local and the global. The process of producing this cross-media event will involve internships: work experience and preparation for entrepreneurship. A team of young people, including early school leavers and students, will conceive, produce and execute the projects themselves.

Collaboration on various levels will elicit an extra reward. Each project will be shown somewhere in Rotterdam public space, for example on a screen or as a projection on a large architectural object, to maximise exposure and let the neighbourhood see its own multiform identity. We hereby seek to position Rotterdam South in the European creative network and to connect youth cultures via the Internet. This will give rise to an international network of creative and cultural initiatives. Its diverse population and critical consumers make Rotterdam South an outstanding laboratory for testing new kinds of productions, products, social innovation and creative entrepreneurship.

How it is developed
The Big South project is the follow-up of the Go-for-IT project, where The Patching Zone set out

to develop a city game for the area of Rotterdam South, the southern part of the city, generally considered a wasteland. During the project, the team made contact with several organizations in the area but more importantly, after using a temporary solution, The Patching Zone rented an office space. More and more this becomes our home base, and is recognized by the neighbourhood: They know we are there and what projects we are responsible for.

The Big South Lab is set up in the Southern area of Rotterdam, where, since several decades, the economy is generally poor and the housing situation bad. Since the end of the 80's, the municipality of Rotterdam invested in the housing situation: big projects replaced the old run down blocks. Later, the South West part of the area was intentionally gentrified: old pieces of the port now have become one of the most luxurious residential areas of the Netherlands.
Still, a couple of yards away, the relatively new housing projects suffer from all the negative effects of immigration, bad education and unemployment. Young people have little choice: they can go either to school and learn a honest but not very profitable profession or stay in the street, where there's a sub-culture, friends and... respect. The third way: articulate your cultural identity and make a profession out of that is seldom successful. The way to the creative industry is usually cut off by lack of knowledge and skills of production technology but also entrepreneurship. Big South is a living lab that uses the experience of the Go-for-it project that The Patching Zone started in 2009 to offer young people from the non-gentrified part of Rotterdam South the means to gain the skills to be independent and at the same time get a spot in the entrepreneurial constellation of the city.

In a way this project has an ambivalent identity: firstly the people of the area are working in a collaborative style with the cultural identity they already had but did not express before in another way and secondly the international team of The Patching Zone is working on a combination of community art, design, cultural work, education, technology and innovation. This mix can be confusing, for all parties involved but can also make the difference between a meaningful project and a mundane, 'creative' project by professional 'do-gooders'.

Examples? Let's work with a generalisation to illustrate this, there's a difference in approach

between a Brazilian and a Dutch person regarding social differences. A Brazillian might think the people of Rotterdam South have all the chances in the world, while a Dutch team member experiences the same people as deprived. The housing-situation for instance in Rotterdam South was considered quite standard by a French team member who is familiar with the 'banlieu's' of Paris.

Context

An important issue in the Big South project was the scaling up of our experiences, to see if the process-patching approach is useful to teach young people. Or should we re-phrase this; it is more useful to teach their teachers to take a different approach, or teach another skill that is more appropriate? It is, of course, easy to fall into the pit of paternalistic top-down attitude, for that style is still frequently used by social workers in the area; 'we know what's best for them, if you leave it to them, you know what will come of it' and has caused a deep distrust of social and other workers in area's like Rotterdam South. It is a lot harder to take the target group seriously, to listen to their wishes and thoughts and to work from there. This means you have to build trust and work together with the target group, to involve people from the target group in the ideation phase of the project. It means the context plays a role that is much more important than in other approaches.

The context of Big South: young people from the area have their own culture, language, music, dance, theatre, food and media, and when you want to involve them in your project you have to hook up with that fact. There's a local dance-style, local Hip Hop flow, a local style of partying and even a local way of promoting parties. If you are into collaboration; look at Rotterdam South. The promotion company works together with the social workers who know the music scene. The music scene collaborates with dancers, video-makers and of course, producers.

Collaboration in any form, is very common. The real problem is they have so little access to the 'outside' world, the world where real money is being made. As long as all these cultural activities take place within the grey economy of trading, they will have a hard time generating money, convince a bank they are solvable etc.

It took us a while to find out where the blank spots are, the issues that are no issues in the 'hood' but are very real outside. We decided communication is for all parties involved crucial but problematic. In general it is relatively easy to reach their own peer group, but a lot more difficult to jump over the wall of your own backyard and talk to the neighbours.

Tools
An important ingredient when starting a project like this is the visibility of the activities and an address where people can find you, which represents your presence in the neighbourhood. Although many of the team members were accustomed to working alone at home and take responsibility, it was imperative to show the neighbourhood we worked together in our 'office'. It took a while, but finally the people of Rotterdam South knew where we are located and what we do.
A good deal of the ideation phase was spent on deciding what tools, what hardware the team would invest in and what could be borrowed or rented. The team researched the possibility of buying a van that could be converted in a mobile lab but this proved to be to time-consuming in the long run. Also it appeared that there was already a bus like this that the team could rent at a reasonable price. Most of the hardware the team uses is rented and/or borrowed. This is more flexible. Also, because the project is a work in progress, it is likely that it's more practical to buy 'tools' (camera's, software etc.) when the projects are up scaled.

Collaboration
The team consisted partly of Patching Zone participants who also took part in the Go-for-IT project. This worked out positively; they were already familiar with the area and the methodology of The Patching Zone.
Much of the methodology is inherently attributed to the project in the way it is set up: a small international team, living near or in the area they work for, involving the user actively in the programme. Some of the methodology is hidden in the way the project is lead or what decisions are taken. The collaboration of the team consisted of roughly four phases: **Concept, Production, Workshops, Up scaling.**

Concept/ideation
As mentioned, team members partly already knew each other, on the other hand there were members that were completely new to a. this kind of collaboration and b. The Netherlands and its cultural values. This has its repercussions on the ideation phase.

In the ideation, several methods were used but most of the decisions were made with a practical approach; these are our targets, these are the possible strategies to reach these targets. We research the possibilities and use the most plausible. Also the budget and feasibility in general was an element that played a decisive role. So we have to chose for creative, yet durable and unorthodox solutions.

Another factor were our partners. We have regular meetings with our partners, these consist of a large number of organisations from the neighbourhood, some commissioning, some partners and some supporting. All these organisations are involved in the ideation process to come to a project plan that is of interest for all. First of all, Pact op Zuid, our commissioner is interested in economic output parameters, such as entrepreneurship and education for the youth. Secondly we collaborated closely with Kosmopolis Rotterdam, an organisation that stimulates cultural exchange and understanding. The footprint of this organisation is visible in the topics of a number of our workshops; for instance the remixing of cultural values is a recurring theme in our curriculum, as is the articulation of your cultural background within predominant culture in the neighbourhood. Combining these different interest fields often turns out to be a challenge, especially the translation of these objectives, which stems from an outsiders perspective on the local target group (the insiders), this required our full attention.

In the ideation phase the skills and academic context of the team members was assessed and the personal goals of the members were articulated. From there, a project plan was drawn up, that gave a clear direction to the final event and set out a curriculum with all targets articulated and an overview of how we wanted to achieve these goals.

Production

In the production phase the team decided that it would be practical to use a mobile centre that facilitates a number of technologies and can be used in almost any given situation. The idea of building a bus with all technology was abandoned, it was estimated as too much work, also because there was an alternative in Frequency, a bus that was already completely rebuilt for our purposes by another organisation that was willing to rent is out to us at a fair price. This left time and money to prepare workshops. The Big South project presented 4 different workshops in the Rotterdam South area:

1   music, beat-making
2   wearables
3   video making
4   augmented reality

For the production, a team member was fully engaged in all practicalities and this worked out fine, also because this was a Dutch-speaking team member.

Workshops/final event

It was a rainy springtime in Rotterdam, especially on the days The Patching Zone planned its activities. This caused little audience attendance on several events and de-motivation from the team. On the other hand we attracted a large number of young people when it was not raining and the brand Patching Zone was gaining momentum: the neighbourhood starts to recognize us and knows what is going on.

The old school bus The Patching Zone used proved to be able to attract a good crowd: enough people to participate in our programme. At the time of writing, the workshops are still going on, but at the horizon there's the final event where all the threads of the project come together.

It is still an open question whether people from the neighbourhood and especially our target group can see the long term effect of the activities that ultimately lead to a final presentation where the results of all separate workshops are shown. We often noticed that young people take an open ended process for granted while we work towards the projects' apotheoses ..... The final phase will, of course, depend on the enthusiasm of our team and participants.

Up scaling/Wrap up

Collaborative projects with a large number of stakeholders (please have a look at the list of our partners) are challenging and sometimes though. Establishing one self as a creative lab in a deprived area takes time, patience and improvisation. Observing a mobile studio full with beat-making youngsters is encouraging...

AUGMENTED REALITY
WORKSHOP

Working in a team and ownership

Georgios Papadakis

Georgios Papadakis is an Installation artist and live electronics performer. He received his education in Music Technology at the University of Hertfordshire (UK). Apart from being a team member at The Patching Zone, Georgios does a research internship at the electronic music lab STEIM in Amsterdam.

At The Patching Zone, Georgios got involved in the Big South Lab about halfway through the project. He moved from Delft, where he lived temporarily, to Rotterdam and took it upon himself to organize the final event of the Big South project. Here's the account of his first couple of months at The Patching Zone.

When I joined the Big South Lab in April 2010, I was rather intimidated by the multitude of professional backgrounds of the team members. Although I had experience with international projects, it was somewhat unclear to me how things were organized and run.
At the same time I had just moved to Rotterdam and was only slightly aware of the characteristics

and qualities of the culture of the local youth, the target group of our project and this increased my initial hesitance on how to connect with them. I needed time to adapt, even though I anticipated on working in the field with a different culture and social group.

Arranging a workshop or event by default involves many stages and dozens of separate tasks. From research and planning to production and documentation. The allocation of the tasks amongst the team members initially appeared unclear to me. I'm used to a strictly task-based approach where a project is divided in distinct parts and assigned to 'owners'. At The Patching Zone, many of the tasks were performed in close co-operation with each other, especially where it concerned the content, everybody was involved equally.

Apart from that, when I joined the team, a series of workshops was already running, so I found myself facing two main challenges: firstly grasping the way the team worked and how tasks were assigned and performed, secondly understanding the methods and scopes of the running project, the background of the participants and offering creative input and support to the rest of the team.

Although puzzled at first, things became much clearer a few days later, during an informal presentation of each team member's past productions. Discussing the projects each of us had been involved in, revealed our particular skills and artistic interests. This had its influence on the design of the current and coming workshops and events.

Also, finding common aesthetic values between our works was a stimulus for the team and created the trust that is necessary for the success of a creative team both concerning the artistic/ stylistic aspects as well as well as the production management. The effect of this presentation and the consequent discussions became valuable for the execution of the Big South Lab: non central tasks were carried out by open-ended co-operations between team members, who both bring and acquire skills and shape collectively the end result, while the division of central tasks was decided by the team in group meetings. This process provides know-how and creative ideas along the way, and because there's a lot of informal communication, the chance of misunderstandings is minimized.

For my part, the long term result was a lesson in constructive project management, as in my experience collective works have a tendency to fall apart when team members are not included in the creative process. I had practical experience with collective task division and performance, and its wholesome consequences for the progress of each part of the project.

André de Groot

Interview by Sam Nemeth

André de Groot, Rotterdam Development Corporation (OBR), works since 2009 for the economical department of the city of Rotterdam and runs development programmes.

How did you get introduced to The Patching Zone?

Since 2009 I work for the Economic Development Department of the city of Rotterdam and especially in the programs for the economical development of the southern part of the city. The Patching Zone was already active when I arrived there. But it was quite unclear to me what The Patching Zone was about so I organized a couple of meetings with director Anne Nigten. I came to the conclusion it is a dynamic organisation with a strong grassroots vantage point: they actually go to the streets where it's happening and start from there. I must say I did not understand all of it but the mix appealed to me.

Because I'm responsible for the Pact op Zuid programme (development of the southern part of Rotterdam) I thought it necessary to get more detailed information about what

The Patching Zone does in this city and the method they're using. So I decided to make it a priority to spend more time to get to know The Patching Zone. I wanted to find out what connections with projects in and outside of our programmes could be made.

In the past months these connections proved easy to realize and they worked out positively for all parties involved. Not only the effects to external parties became apparent but also inside the programme, projects became more visible because of these crossovers.

What is the actual result of the Patching Zone projects for an economic programme like Pact op Zuid?

I think the most interesting result is the mix of young people from the street and high-end technology. Combined with co-operations with international universities, these projects are a powerful tool for social and economical innovation.

The Patching Zone is an incubator where talent that arrives directly from the street develops and gains more perspective to contribute economically to this city. The beauty is that young people get introduced to skills that will be important in the near future and get handed a roadmap for the use of these skills in an economical model. And that is usually what makes projects like this successful: the combination of creative power and the possibility for talents to realize ambitions.

How do you see the long-term effects of the presence of an organisation like the Patching Zone in the area of Rotterdam Zuid?

Well, the mere fact that there's a 'node', a centre of all sorts of activities, of course does have impact. And I mean not only the effect on the young people that have a direct relationship with The Patching Zone, but also the repercussions that this has on their own circles, on their own social context. There's a growing awareness that new media is relatively easy to access and a tool to realize your cultural, artistic or economic idea's.

This is our core business: the stimulation of economical dynamics. But that's not where I think the primary focus of The Patching Zone lies, although it is undoubtedly part of their work. I think The Patching Zone convinces, by their approach, young people that they have talent, and that it is important to show their talent, and also that the tools to do all this are not far away and easy to use. That is the most important long-term effect of The Patching Zone in Rotterdam Zuid: giving young people the conviction their culture and their creativity is the most valuable thing they have. Something to be proud of.

The Patching Zone uses the processpatching method of Anne Nigten. What makes this method different from other methods and/or organisations?

Well that's actually an interesting subject because it is something we discussed a lot. The Patching Zone, the way I see it, works from the

user perspective. The Patching Zone occupies a little bit of space in an area where a project is likely to take place and then the Patching Zone team first sits and waits to see what happens. The ideas have to come from the people in the area themselves. But there has to be trust that something positive will come from this. What you add a little bit of management and a method and that makes the ultimate difference. The starting point is, as in any good creative design process, the user. The funny thing is that you need actually very little ingredients to get these processes going.

The Processpatching method is in itself also an element that I would like to see distributed over our other projects. I see it as a way of collaboration in projects, profitable for every stakeholder. The user, the target group of a project, gains, apart from the results of the project, awareness of the skills and tools available. The

international project team gets an intensive crash course in trans local collaboration. The local partners who are involved in the project get introduced to new ways of project management and collaboration. And that's something that used to be unthinkable: a project that is positive for everybody involved. I think the time is ready..

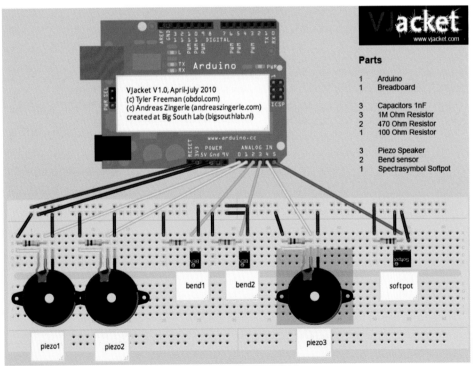

VJacket

Andreas Zingerle
and Tyler Freeman

The VJacket is a wearable controller for live video performance. Built into this old bomber jacket are all kinds of sensors to control visuals on the screen; hit sensors, light sensors, bend sensors and touch sliders that allow you to control video effects and transitions, trigger clips and scratch frames all from the comfort of your own jacket. This way, the VJ is freed from the boring, cumbersome interface of mouse and keyboard, and instead can use the very clothes on his body to control the video and sound with a precise dance converting convulsing limbs into luscious light shows. Each sensor sends fully customizable OpenSoundControl or MIDI messages wirelessly over Bluetooth to the VJ program of your choice using the Arduino2OSC bridge.

The Arduino2OSC bridge interface we developed for Arduino projects can send any type of OSC message to any program, including other video or audio programs, such as Resolume Avenue, Arkaos Grand VJ, Reaktor, Propellerheads Reason, Supercollider, Max/MSP, etc. Thus you can use the VJacket to not only control video, but sound and other networked interactive media as well. All the code and hardware design is open source so others can make their own wearable controllers to contribute to the growing wave of performative fashion.

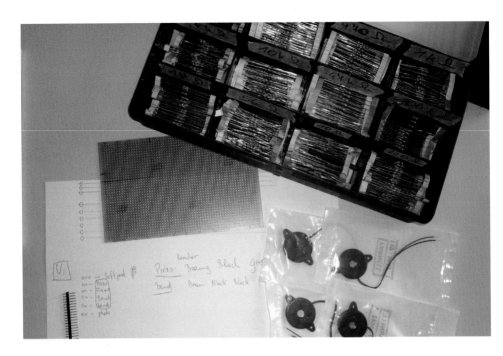

Technical Implementation

The VJacket uses a Bluetooth Arduino microcontroller board to wirelessly relay the sensor data to the computer. To take it from there, we built the Arduino2OSC bridge: an easily configurable graphical interface that creates customizable OpenSoundControl messages from the sensor data. It also allows you to adjust the analog input data from the Arduino to your exact needs – scaling input and output values, adding cutoff thresholds, etc. – with enough options to (hopefully) cover all your Arduino input requirements; no matter if your sensor is a continuous slider or a one-hit piezo contact mic, no matter if you are manipulating a video effect or triggering audio samples, we tried to make it flexible enough so you're not stuck reprogramming a new patch for every project - just make a new preset and you're done

For our first video demo, we used the VJacket through Arudino2OSC to send Open Sound Control messages to Resolume Avenue, a popular VJ program. The Arduino2OSC bridge interface is generic enough to send any type of OSC or MIDI message to any program that accepts them, including other video or audio programs like Arkaos Grand VJ, Max/MSP/Jitter, Reaktor, Abelton Live, Propellerheads Reason, Supercollider, Kyma, Processing, OpenFrameworks, etc. You can even send the messages over the LAN for networked performances!

We will soon make available the circuit designs, Arduino code, and Arduino2OSC Max/MSP patch/application – all under an open source license – so stay tuned to make your own VJacket!

Kevin Brito

Interview by Sam Nemeth

Kevin Brito joined The Patching Zone as an intern from 'De Nieuwe Kans', an institution in the Rotterdam Zuid area that literally gives people 'a new chance'. Kevin is a dancer but discovered more talents during his period at The Patching Zone: he is a gifted graphic artist and will go to the Rotterdam Graphics School (Grafisch Lyceum) in February 2011.

I heard about The Patching Zone at 'De Nieuwe Kans' and joined a workshop at an early stage. A little bit later, when I realized i had to work on my creative talents and understood more what The Patching Zone was about, I joined

the team and started working on a portfolio whilst working on the Go-for-IT! project.

Later I joined the Big South project but then I was already a different man. You cannot believe how much The Patching Zone changed me; the fact that the people there appreciate what I do and recognize my talent and also who I am, gives me such a good feeling, there's nothing like it. When people tell me I did well, that still gives me a huge kick. That's something I learned at The Patching Zone.

Did your way of expressing yourself also change?

That I don't know but I'm sure that the team's trust in me makes me feel good. When I have trouble, The Patching Zone people help me, it is a little bit like a second family.

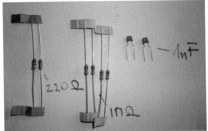

Was it also like this in the beginning ?

I was impressed by all these different people from all over the world but they made me feel welcome from the start. And also the feedback from my friends and family was positive. They saw that I found something that was good for me. I participate in projects from my expertise as a dancer and feel recognized like that. On the other hand I learn, not only skills like drawing or working with the computer, but also how to work together with people and of course my English has greatly improved.

Are you ready for your new step at the graphics school?

I do not know if I'm really ready but I feel I'm definitely more experienced, more mature than a couple of years ago. I have the ability to work together with people from different cultures and what's more important, i feel good about myself.

Partners:

 Ministerie van Onderwijs, Cultuur en Wetenschap

Ministerie van Economische Zaken

De Nieuwe Kans ■ ■

Conclusion

Anne Nigten

I would like to conclude this book with some reflections. First I'll briefly revisit parts of our way of working followed by a brief summary of our most used Processpatching aspects as outlined in the first chapters of this book. Some highlighted loose threads and untouched issues will follow this and I'll end with our future plans.

General observations

First, I'll briefly highlight our most used Processpatching aspects or research approaches based on our practice: Playing and Making as drivers for our research and development and audience participation. Playing as research turned out to be a valid approach to get acquainted with the local peers and stakeholders in an informal setting. We frequently used playing as a vehicle to understand the context, the people and their interests. Playing provided the team with information that is hard to reveal through questionnaires or interviews. The game testing events in the Go for IT! project for example, provided us with information about game preferences and, this is very useful, how the local target group likes to play or how the local youth uses their mobile phones. These playful tests informed us on two levels: for the technical part and the user's perspective. In several events we noticed that playing serves as a perfect icebreaker for people, with different educational and cultural backgrounds, to get to know each other by playing together. Fun and immersion are keywords here to enter alternative realities. Making is an other useful approach to create shared experiences, the materials work as boundary objects to bridge interests, expertise and gives access to personal conversations. Both playing and making are crucial ingredients for practice lead research, as it enables us to fully engage with our stakeholders and provides room to include their interest and/or skills in the next phase of the development cycle. Both playing and making are useful as placeholders to bridge research and the real world in multiple directions. It informs our teams while engaging with their target group and peers.

Playing and making are both essential ingredients to establish audience participation. The seeds for co-creation and co-ownership are grown in our playing and making workshops. The people that were formerly known as end users, have helped us anchor our collaboration model in real life. We often refer to them as stakeholders while their role in the projects develops from guides towards peers and co-owners, this has added an additional and very important layer in the Processpatching collaboration scheme. In theory this might appear complicated, though it proved direct feedback is a key to their engagement. The given situation in which we work, in combination with the international team members' sincere interest in the local community, brings forward plenty of inspiration and new insights. Our preference to have the team members embedded in the work area (on-site), results in very interesting exchanges between the local stakeholders and The Patching Zone's participants. There is an interest to learn from each other's cultural and creative backgrounds. As you read earlier we often organize introduction tours to get our people acquainted with the work environment. However, the real life tours are guided by the local stakeholders and are driven by the shared interests among them and our team members. What might be worthwhile to mention as a learnt lesson here is the cliché that trust takes time; understanding the local social tapestry, the habits and how one could fit in or contribute with something sensible takes time and careful attention.

Issues that were not explicitly addressed

Sustainability
Sustainability has many different meanings, for the moment I'll focus on sustainability as the long-term effect of our projects and how we enable the stakeholders, commissioners or successors to continue our work or at the least learn from it. The emotional or inspirational footprint we leave behind in the hearts of people is not to be measured or registered so we therefore fall back to known measuring tools from, among others, ethnography and design practice. Besides documentation and descriptive reflections as you read in this book, our teams also wrote manuals that were left behind for the future; for example the Recycle-X project made a small booklet

with all kinds of manuals, based on their work in Dordrecht. These cover the broad range of activities they have been engaged in, we find here new soup recipes, manuals for urban gardening, manuals for recycling, how-to's for making your own lead installation and making plants talk. This range of diverse topics illustrates the complexity of measuring the outcomes on a longer term. The beauty of new insights during the project's course is a complication for measuring the results in a quantitative way. In the Cultuur Lokaal project we worked with a base line measurement, provided by the Dutch Telematics Institute (these days called: Novay.nl) that was updated quarterly. Here the effect of our project on the professional activities was taken as the guideline. The results were very positive, the project had a high ranking and the funding bodies were pleased. However, these measurements were abstract and far removed from the daily practice of our trainees: the cultural heritage staff. Our partners therefore decided to make a small booklet that provided an overview of the project and its results from the trainees (stakeholders) perspective (Kuiper, E., Rijken, D., 2008). The making of the booklet worked as a reflection and self-evaluation on the participatory process while some parts fell in place for the cultural heritage participants during the book making process. The team's contributions on all projects also reflects the time needed for scientific writing, while Cultuur Lokaal is long time passed, the Big South Lab project is still under construction and its reflections are not there yet.

From the first Patching Zone project our work has been included in the project observatory, a project database initiated by the Virtueel Platform, the Dutch E-culture sector institute. Our work, the process and progress of the projects, is documented through interviews and external observations. This provides an extensive monitoring report on our work that has been mapped out in detail. Recently Liesbeth Huybrechts (University of Genk and PhD candidate at the Catholic University Leuven in Belgium) started on the extension of these external observations by analyses of the Go for IT! and Big South Lab projects. As most of our projects are limited in time, we are happy with these reflective collaborations after the completion of our projects. As one might understand our commissioners often have to focus on the concrete outcomes and cannot afford extensive long-term scientific research, although most of them acknowledge the relevance of our work for developing broader insights and aggregated expertise on, for example, economic, creative and cultural knowledge. For most of our projects we engage therefore with academic partners to collaborate on the project's aftermath and we are always interested in new partnerships in this field.

Social aspects in teams

An issue we did not emphasis in the book is the social mechanisms of the project teams. As one can probably imagine, the personality match among several unknown people is not easy to read from application forms, and much harder to extract from a resume than competences or expertise. For example, a team can be composed of the most talented people but wouldn't work without the interest and courage of all its members to open ones self up for real exchange. We

noticed that it is of crucial importance for the team members to leave behind ones own, built in, desire for controlling the process in one's personal (and probably often proven as useful) way. We also observed that this turns out to be especially difficult in the start-up phase of a project. As this will always have its repercussions when the project proceeds, we pay special attention to a respectful and open collaboration early in the project. Based on our earlier experiences we did consider to take more drastic or hilarious measures that could contribute to the collaborative creative results, for example we discussed the option of observation cameras and real life documentary approaches for analyzing the process. For multiple (ethical and practical) reasons this has not been realized so far. I'm bringing this to the fore, as it touches the core of our business and is often a focal point of our attention. We cannot provide a simple blueprint yet, as we need to run more projects before we can draw trustworthy conclusions here.

For the remaining issues that were not addressed we are open to have a conversation with you or hope to provide answers in the next volume.

Next steps

The content of this book reveals only certain parts of our work in a more or less, qualitative manner. We could have hours of conversation about the do's and don'ts, beautiful stories and social, practical and creative insights that might be of relevance to other initiatives that work in urban redevelopment areas, creative industry or user driven design. Instead we are considering facilitating this knowledge transfer based on our projects in real life by adding an expertise service to our work. As this knowledge is event specific and extremely dynamic, we are currently studying how The Patching Zone could become a 'real projects for real people knowledge centre' that bridges academic, creative research with real life situations.

The first two years of The Patching Zone have lead us to the results as outlined in this volume, and the above mentioned attention points, which are all part of a dynamic 'processpatching' process that still grows and develops. Every time, each project and each team creates a unique series of patches that resembles its process, it's knowledge and its people. This experience and knowledge has learnt us about our strength and showed us where we could extend our work as a transdisciplinairy catalyst for creative innovation. Over the last two years we have grown from the new kid on the block into a well-oiled organisation that can fully engage in creative R&D projects with a focus on user driven design. Our quality flourishes best in the early phases of transformation trajectories where people are sought to participate and to engage, as our work is people driven not technology driven.

These two years also lead us to revisit our general research objectives. In the next years we plan to focus on two main research themes; urban transformation processes (creative research as a catalyst for engaged social and economic growth and ecological development) and training for the more conventional art sector whom we aim to assist in order to prepare their professional work for the second half of the 21st century.

References:
Virtueel Platform, project observatory
www.virtueelplatform.nl/projectobservatory
www.map-it.be/
Kuiper, E., Rijken, D., eds. Buiten Spelen, Haagse Hogeschool and Waterwolf publishers (NL), 2008
www.novay.nl/en/

Biografies

Andreas.Muk.Haider (AT) is a media artist and cameraman from Austria, working in Vienna. He graduated recently at the University of Applied Arts, Vienna in digital art and was an exchange student at Willem de Kooning Academy in Rotterdam, NL. He is founding member of tagR. tv-association for media art. He works as a freelance cameraman/assistant and directed numerous documentary films, video performances and video installations that were shown at festivals worldwide. Andreas. Muk.Haider participated in the Go for IT! project.

Andreas Zingerle (AT), is a media artist and designer. He holds a master degree from the University of Art and Industrial Design, Linz, Austria (department of Media Theory – Interface Cultures). In spring 2008, he did an exchange semester at the Media Lab, Taideteollinen korkeakoulu (University of Art and Design), Helsinki/Finland. His interactive installations and experimental videos are frequently shown in international festivals. Andreas participated in Go for IT! and the Big South Lab project. More information: www.andreaszingerle. com

----

Anne Nigten (PhD) (NL) is the director of The Patching Zone. Prior to her current position, she was the manager of V2_Lab, the aRt&D department of V2_, Institute for the Unstable Media in Rotterdam, the Netherlands. She is adviser for several media art and science initiatives in the Netherlands and Europe. She completed her PhD at the University of the Arts London (UK). She frequently lectures and publishes papers on art, engineering and (computer) science collaboration.

Christopher Baronavski (US) is a designer, programmer, and filmmaker, and has studied at the College of William & Mary in Virginia

and Parsons School of Design in New York City. He is currently completing a graduate degree in the Lens-Based Media programme at the Piet Zwart Instituut, Willem de Kooning Academie, in Rotterdam.

Corinna Pape (DE) is a researcher and assistant lecturer at the Department of Communication Studies at Otto-von-Guericke University of Magdeburg, Germany. Her research focuses on how mobile and locative interfaces shape people's interactions in urban spaces and create new forms of engagement, storytelling and creativity. She holds a PhD in Performance and Media Studies from the Goethe University of Frankfurt am Main and teaches classes on locreativity, performance tactics and digital culture. Corinna participated in the Cultuur Lokaal project.

Georgios Papadakis (GR) is an interactive installation artist and live electronics performer. He studied Music Technology (BSc Honours) at University of Hertfordshire and Philosophy in Film at Edinburgh Open University. He has composed for music theatre and contemporary dance. Georgios currently holds a research assistant position at STEIM institute and participates at the Big South Lab project.

Lyndsey Housden (UK/NL) is an artist and producer based in The Hague, NL. She holds an MA in ArtScience from The Royal Conservatoire, NL, and BA Hons in Fine Art Intermedia from Kingston University, UK. Her work focuses on the physical and psychological effects of space, architecture and social interaction she often collaborates with dancers, architects and artists. Lyndsey Housden was production coordinator at The Patching Zone from 2008 to 2010

Javier Busturia (ES) is an artist working on site-specific interventions related to territory involving communities, focused on collaborative and collective projects. He graduated from the Facultad de Bellas Artes of Universidad Complutense de Madrid (Spain), completing his final year at Kunsthøgskolen i Bergen (Norway). He is a Master in Art Production by the Universidad Politécnica de Valencia (Spain), currently developing is PhD on participatory landscape at UPV. Javier participated in the Recycle-X project in Dordrecht from January to August 2010.

Jelle Dekker (NL) is a student at the Depart-ment of Industrial Design, Eindhoven University of Technology (TU/e) with a focus on new interactive and intelligent product/system design. Also photographer and web-designer, see www.jelledekker.com. He is interested in working together with the user and community and how a design can fit into its environment while triggering interaction from people. Jelle participated as an intern for the Recycle-X project.

Jingni Wang (CN), born in 1986, is a Shanghai based artist. She received her bachelor degree at the New Media Art Department, China Academy of Art in 2009, and from October 2010 she will start her graduate study in the school of Cross Media Art, China Academy of Art. She works with community organizations in Shanghai and is interested in the impact art brings to the spirit of community. Jingni Wang participated the Recycle-X project in Dordrecht in 2010.

Kristina Andersen (DK/NL) is a maker and researcher. She holds an MA in Design, an M.Sc in Virtual Environments, and was a research fellow at the Interaction Design Institute Ivrea.

She has taught and mentored at institutions like DasArts, Piet Zwart Institute, Willem de Kooning Academie and hosted numerous informal workshops in strange locations. She is currently thinking about tangible sensing strategies and magical thinking. Kristina is a mentor at The Patching Zone and research director at STEIM in Amsterdam.

Matthew Fuller (UK) works at the Centre for Cultural Studies, Goldsmiths, University of London, and was previously at the Piet Zwart Institute, Rotterdam. His books include 'Media Ecologies, materialist energies in art and technoculture', 'Behind the Blip, essays on the culture of software'. He is editor of 'Software Studies, a lexicon', and co-editor of the new Software Studies series from MIT Press. He was a member of The Patching Zone supervisory board from inception until 2010.

Mirella Misi (BR) is a choreographer, videomaker and researcher. Graduated in Dance on the Dance Department of the Federal University of Bahia-Brazil. Master and PhD in Performing Arts on the field of Art and Technology at the Theatre School of the Federal University of Bahia-Brazil. She participated in the Cultuur Lokaal Project.

Nancy Mauro-Flude (AU) media-designer and performing-artist. Alumni of DasArts: advanced institute for dance/theatre, and graduate of Piet Zwart Institute – Media Design. PhD candidate and Lecturer at School of Art, University of Tasmania. Founder of Moddr @WORM. She engages with computer sub-culture in a speculative manner & questions how information systems are having an impact on our embodiment. Her research about this vital crossover contributed to FLOSS+Art (London: Mute Publishing). Nancy participated in Cultuurlokaal, The Patching Zone's pilot project.

Pinar Temiz (TR) works as a musician, singer/songwriter and sound designer with a music technology background. She is Experienced in sound installations and interactive sound design. Throughout her education she worked on sound design in various contexts such as games, films and performance arts (specifically contemporary dance). She recently started her Master studies at Utrecht School of the Arts in the Netherlands. Pinar participated in the Go for IT! and Big South Lab projects.

Rene Wassenburg (NL) is a hardware developer and runs Schrikdraad Elektronisch Ontwerp, an electronics design company based in the Netherlands, he collaborates mostly with artists, performers, and organizations working in the field of new media. Rene worked as a hardware mentor for the Go for IT! and the Big South Lab project.

Ricardo Nascimento (BR) works as artist, multimedia developer and producer. He received his Master in arts at the KunstuniversitaÄàt Linz (AT) in the Interface Culture Department and graduated in International Relations by PUC-SP and Multimedia Design by Art Center SENAC-SP in Brasil. He participated in many festivals and exhibitions in Asia, Europe and America and he has been the recipient of several awards. Ricardo participated in the Recycle-X project. More info at www.popkalab.com

----

Sam Nemeth (NL) studied Film and Television (now called Media and Culture) at UvA. He worked with the video collective Staats – TV Rabotnik, and for the educational department of the Stedelijk Museum in Amsterdam. He was editor of the Dutch AV magazine Skrien. He held several functions at medialab Waag Society in Amsterdam. Apart from this he works as a freelance documentary

maker and writing journalist. Sam Nemeth is currently lecturer/coach at The University of Eindhoven and is staff member of trans disciplinary medialab The Patching Zone in Rotterdam. Sam is mentor of the Big South Lab project. personal blog: www.klemspot.blogspot.com, current project at The Patching Zone: www.bigsouthlab.nl/

Sietse Dols (NL) is a designer who is currently finishing his bachelor degree at the Industrial Design faculty of the Technical University Eindhoven. Sietse completed his bachelor internship at The Patching Zone where he was involved in the Go for IT! and Big South Lab projects.

Simon de Bakker (NL) is a software and hardware engineer and is exploring the fields of embedded technologies, smart textiles and soft-sensor design. He holds a BSc in Interaction Design and an MA in Interactive Multi-Media at the School for the Arts Utrecht. Simon works for V2_lab, and since 2009 as a technical mentor and developer for The Patching Zone.

Vivian Wenli Lin (TW/US) is a Taiwanese-American video artist who focuses on creating media portraits of women to give voices to marginalized communities. She received a Bachelor's degree in Psychology and Asian American Studies at U.C. Berkeley (US). In 2008, and her Masters in Fine Arts at the Sandberg Instituut in Amsterdam (NL). She is the founder and co-director of the foundation, Voices of Women Media. She participated in the Cultuur Lokaal project.

Art Center College Library
1700 Lida Street
Pasadena, CA 91103